BEATING THE ODDS

PRAISE FOR *BEATING THE ODDS*

"*Beating the Odds* is a book that young and old alike should read. It is encouraging and insightful, as well as a teaching tool for all those who happen to see life as 'a glass half empty.'"

Mila Mulroney, Honorary Director, Cystic Fibrosis Canada

"We could all use a little more resiliency: *Beating the Odds* is the perfect guide to getting it."

Amanda Lang, Anchor, BNN Bloomberg, and best-selling author of *Power of Why* and *Beauty of Discomfort*

"Chris MacLeod shows us the remarkable strength of the human spirit in *Beating the Odds*. His lessons are an inspiration to anyone looking to overcome hardship in their life."

Frank Stronach, Founder, Magna International Inc., Chairman, Stronach International Inc., and author of *The Magna Man*, *The Question of All Questions*, and *The Greed Factor*

"I have personally witnessed the power of Chris's optimism and resilience. Whatever the odds you're working against, Chris will inspire you to overcome them."

Sheila Copps, Former Deputy Prime Minister of Canada and author of *Nobody's Baby*

"I have witnessed the caring, the passion and the hard work of Chris MacLeod since 1989 when he started working with us on Parliament Hill. I have seen his resilience over the years. Chris makes the impossible possible. This book is a must read."

Dennis Mills, Former Member of Parliament for Toronto-Danforth

"One of my favourite quotes is from Elon Musk who once told an interviewer that, '*When something is important enough you do it even if the odds aren't in your favour*'. It's that mindset that got us to the moon and back, that discovered insulin and that developed a Covid-19 vaccine in less than 10 months. Chris MacLeod is the walking definition of what Musk is talking about … and he is changing the odds for people with cystic fibrosis."

Dan Donovan, Publisher & Managing Editor, *Ottawa Life Magazine*

"I often think of Chris as an insightful warrior. He is driven, committed and always inspiring. Chris is where he is, health-wise, not only because of advancements in science, but importantly because of his attitude and approach to life and living. This book will be helpful to people living with cystic fibrosis and other diseases – but frankly his advice is helpful to us all."

Kelly Grover, CEO, Cystic Fibrosis Canada

"I could write a book about the impact of this book. At the very moment Chris bestowed his hard-won wisdom and sage practicality to me, I was afraid to lose my life and the battle meant facing a wall of Goliaths — a whole government, a global pharmaceutical company, and the media … just for starters. 'We have to get in war mode,' he told me, and for the first time, I had guidance from someone who had been in the trenches like me. Chris's guidance dropped the sugar-coating, and got to the gritty strategy I needed to win. It led me to victory. I could say this book saved my life, and it would be literal. Here's what is even better: this book gave me the strength to save my own."

Lilia Zaharieva, Advocate and lead representative plaintiff in the first class action on behalf of CF patients in Canada

"There is nothing more exhilarating than 'Beating the Odds' when you've been dealt a truly lousy hand. And to do it time after time! Now I know why Chris MacLeod is on a perpetual high. Thanks for sharing your formula for a 'never better' daily life experience. You are an inspiration to all."

Durhane Wong-Rieger, President & CEO, Canadian Organization for Rare Disorders

"Chris MacLeod knows what he speaks. He is not only a CF warrior but he has helped so many as a CF lawyer. We as a community are grateful for people like Chris who know what it takes to advocate for those who want their voices heard."

Andy Lipman, Author and founder of the *CF Warrior Project*
Atlanta, Georgia

"I have watched Chris's indomitable spirit triumph over and over again in the most challenging of circumstances. He describes his life in vivid metaphors — for example, a Super Bowl game — where everything is on the line, and one is thrown onto the field with no practice, no experience at all. Chris's lived example — taking control of his *attitude* — can serve as a blueprint for others faced with difficult odds. That attitude spills over into action — a powerful way to 'take charge' when so much is beyond one's control. Jesse Jackson once said 'Both tears and sweat are salty, but they render a different result. Tears will get you sympathy: sweat will get you change.' Chris's story makes it clear that he wants no sympathy. Instead, he chooses to roll up his sleeves and use his considerable gifts to 'sweat' effectively for change."

Patti Tweed, Parent of a person with CF and health advocate

"Chris MacLeod is a warrior for life. He never gives up. Not with a hole in his heart as a newborn; not with the cystic fibrosis which threatens his wellbeing every time he wants to take another breath; not when bleeding from his wracked lungs would not stop for months. Life can be difficult; Chris challenges each of us to be much more than we think we can be. Become the CEO of your health and life. Chris does not take no for an answer, especially from himself. Every person with an unmet health need can be a warrior for life, so no onc is left behind. *Beating the Odds* shares Chris's experiences and reflections, so we all can learn from and then apply by making the next move. And the next. As a thinking person of faith, he frames a dozen lessons for us based on his personal journey. One excerpt: 'I was told the ADM did not meet with individuals. That led me to establish the Canadian Cystic Fibrosis Treatment Society … to advocate for individuals that need access to medicines like Kalydeco. I will leave the rest of this story for another day.' We all need to hear more from Chris on that story. Lives hang in the balance."

John Adams, Chair, Best Medicines Coalition

"*Beating the Odds* is a reminder of the power we have over our lives, no matter the circumstance. Chris balances candid storytelling on the realities living with cystic fibrosis with insightful advice on how to tackle adversity in a tangible and digestible way. This book is one to refer back to again and again – whenever you need some inspiration or guidance on your journey."

Hailey S. Laxer, National Patient Advocate

"Where do I start when speaking of Chris MacLeod? Well I guess at the beginning. Chris came into our lives 10 years ago when we desperately needed a hero. I didn't know Chris and he didn't know my daughter or me. However, he quickly reached out to us to support our effort to battle the government and secure reimbursement for a Cystic Fibrosis modulator my daughter desperately needed. Chris was a *huge* part of our success, without him I am not sure the outcome would have been what it was. Upon meeting him the first thing that struck me was his positivity. He always smiled, and consistently put a positive spin on situations that at times were more than a little frustrating. When no one was there for us, Chris was, and I will always appreciate him for making himself available to answer the constant questions I had for him. Chris continues to be a force in the Cystic Fibrosis community. He has been working for years in an effort to help patients across Canada gain access to lifesaving medications. Whether he is launching a lawsuit to change how patients are able to access medications or flying across the country to support individual advocacy efforts he is in this 100%. Despite a busy and thriving law practice and dealing with Cystic Fibrosis himself, he is always there to help in any way he can. Chris's kindness, positivity and tenacity has inspired advocates across Canada to stand up and use their voice for what is right. Patients see someone who although dealing with the same health challenges they deal with gets up each day with purpose, integrity and gratitude to live a life that he can feel proud of. Chris doesn't wear a cape, but for those that know him, he is a true hero. I will be forever grateful to Chris for his support through our battle and his deep commitment to our community. I feel blessed to be able to call him a friend."

Beth Vanstone, Mother of Madi Vanstone and founding member of CF Get Loud

BEATING THE ODDS

11 Lessons to Overcome a Health Crisis
and Lead a More Resilient Life

CHRIS MACLEOD

BIG SKY
PUBLISHING

Beating The Odds: 11 Lessons to Overcome a Health Crisis and Lead a More Resilient Life, by Chris MacLeod

ISBN 978-1-7775753-0-4

Big Sky Publishing
333 Adelaide Street West
Toronto, Ontario
4th floor M5V 1R5

First printing 2021.

www.beatingtheodds.ca

Book design by Sherpa Creative: Wade Gilpin and Brianna Petz

1 2 3 4 5 25 24 23 22 21

Printed and bound in Canada.

Dedicated to all those who fought the good fight
but were taken too early.

They taught me much, and their memory continues
to inspire and will not soon be forgotten.

CONTENTS

A GUIDE FOR YOU

How to use the 11 lessons as a personal resource for you as you overcome the challenges that you face.

At the end of every chapter we have one page that is meant as a tool for you to write down your own personal thoughts and story.

Every individual has unique challenges. We all have our own mountains to climb. Take a minute and reflect on the lesson you have just read. Then apply it to the facts of your own life.

Take ideas out of your head and put them on paper. In doing so, let inspiration and your intuition guide you. That is always the first step to overcoming what appears to be an insurmountable challenge.

How can you take the current challenges you face, whether with your health, finance, relationships or life, and apply the lessons in this book?

Write down the first thoughts that come to your mind.

As we say in Lesson 5, writing it down is essential to achieving it.

We need to take the ideas in our heads and put them on paper and then tell people about them. No one can help you achieve your goals if they have no idea where you are headed.

We need to write them down to properly articulate them for ourselves.

Every one of us has very real hurdles we need to overcome. To do so we need to cultivate resilience, lean in on focus, discipline and consistency. Sharpen our habits, rituals and routines. Easier said than done. But we need to be constantly looking for, listening to and reading about the experiences of others. Life is about learning. Not just from experience but from others who have walked the same or sometimes a different path. Their stories can be a guide for our own lives if we choose to let it be.

That is why you need to always find a tribe, a team. If you don't know people personally who can help, you will always find them on the shelves of a bookstore.

That's what I have always done. Look for inspiration wherever I can find it: books, shows, videos. With YouTube and the Internet, it's not hard to locate inspiration.

We are richer in resources now than ever before.

The other avenue is the people around you. You can constantly find inspiration from people if you just ask them to tell you their story and then listen intently.

FOREWORD

When I established the Toronto Adult Cystic Fibrosis Clinic almost three decades ago, I did not appreciate the impact that people with CF would have on my philosophy of life. I did not anticipate how I would be stretched as a physician beyond what I studied in medical school. "Patient Advocate" would be added to my job description. Witnessing the lifelong challenges faced by people with CF and their families would influence me as a person and also change what I teach the student physicians about what is really important to patients. As time passes, I realise that these learnings are not specific to medicine, but apply to all aspects of life. In *Beating the Odds: 11 Lessons to Overcome a Health Crisis and Lead A More Resilient Life*, Chris MacLeod has shared his life journey and insights, and how we can apply these messages to our own lives.

To put his story in context, it helps to understand the world of CF 40–50 years ago. The first medical description of CF was in 1938 and the first CF clinics were set up in the late 1950s. CF is a hereditary disease. It is a result of a mutation in a gene that describes how to build a channel that controls movement of salt into and out of cells, which in turn influences the amount of water in our mucus secretions. People with CF have abnormally thick and sticky mucus that blocks various organs, including the lungs, sinuses, digestive tract, and pancreas. Bacteria trapped in lung mucus leads to recurrent chest infections and ultimately an early death.

When Chris was diagnosed with CF, the median age of survival was only four years; half the children born with CF at the time died before they started kindergarten. It is a daunting scenario to imagine: parents confronting CF, having to decide how to respond – should they "ignore" the medical facts and push on, setting quixotic expectations and aim for a "normal" life. As Chris outlines, with every year he lived, the life expectancy would improve a bit, and so he surfed the survival wave and learned that the doctors were not always right in their predictions.

I met Chris when he became a patient at the clinic I established, but I really got to know him when he was admitted to hospital with a serious lung infection that literally left him gasping for breath. Hospitalization is a humbling experience. It takes away so many of the things that are important to us: function, quality of life, and confidence. We lose privacy, dignity, respect based on our outside life, and control. We have little control of big issues like the treatment plan, as well as less significant issues like what and when we will eat. Our confidence is shaken. With every doctor visit, we fear bad news.

But Chris was different. He took back control. He wanted to know: what is the plan for today? He emailed me to set up an "appointment" for my daily visit. He dressed for my visit like it was a business meeting, and he behaved like he was the CEO. He clearly had expectations of me and my team. His goals were written on the whiteboard in his room. We were accountable to him for his medical treatment. This was a very unusual patient!

What I did not appreciate at the time was his approach to life and health was an example of the Stoic philosophy, as articulated by Marcus Aurelius 2,000 years ago. We cannot change what is out of our control, but we can change how we respond. We should aim to live a good life, to maximize positive thoughts and happiness, and reduce negative emotions. Chris's life story illustrates this philosophy with anecdotes of people with CF that he has met over the years. Although their health struggles may be more than we have had to face, these extraordinary individuals provide us with an example of how to approach life.

A decade ago, Chris was the first person in Canada to gain access to a new class of medications called CFTR modulators. He was able to commence therapy with ivacaftor (brand name: Kalydeco) at a time in his life when he was critically ill. His return to health sparked his goal to help other people with CF access these life-saving medications. Well, perhaps spark is the wrong image – Chris's response was like a rocket! He has used his education and position, as well as his perseverance, to gain the ear of politicians and has been a leading figure in the drive to improve the quantity and quality of life for people with CF. I know first-hand what it is like to be caught up in his energy and drive, to find myself beside him in a press conference at Queen's Park, speaking up to effect change.

Cystic Fibrosis looks different now. The future is brighter, with drug development targeting the basic defect of CF and the hope of preventing organ damage before it occurs. But we have not reached the finish line yet. These drugs are not available for all patients and people with CF continue to die too young. The fight continues and brave warriors, like Chris, will provide an example of the way to live. Chris's life lessons – to maintain positivity, to take charge of your life, to dream, to write, to act, to smile, to get up, to dress up, to show up, to never give up, and to be "never better" – are inspirational and applicable to us all, at all times, perhaps no more so than now as we struggle with a global COVID-19 pandemic.

Elizabeth Tullis MD, FRCPC

Founding Director, Toronto Adult CF Clinic, St Michael's Hospital
Professor of Medicine, University of Toronto,
Toronto, 2021

INTRODUCTION

This book – arising from the lessons I've learned dealing with my lifelong health crisis – is a guide to assist others surviving their own unique health challenges and crises. More than that, it can be a guide to living a full and authentic life.

First, a bit about me, my health story, and an important acknowledgement: I have been blessed with a life far longer than anyone would have anticipated when I entered this world on 29 September 1969, at 4:05 in the afternoon.

About a week later my parents realized something was drastically wrong. I was limp and unresponsive. I was taken to the hospital, and was found to be in heart failure. I was immediately admitted to the Montreal Children's Hospital neonatal intensive care unit, where I spent the next few weeks.

After various investigations I was found to have a large hole between two chambers of my heart – the cause of the heart failure. Because I was only six pounds, it was decided that I was not a good candidate for heart surgery, given the techniques that were available at that time. I was treated with Digitalis, a common medication to strengthen contractions of the heart muscle.

The hope was that the hole in my heart would become smaller with age. Given a 50% chance of survival, I made it past the finish line that was forced upon me.

This would be only the opening act in a lifetime of beating the odds.

As I grew older, my heart problems seemed less prominent, although the condition did require ongoing treatment, including antibiotics whenever I had a cold. For a time, this drew attention away from the other health challenge that I would end up fighting on an ongoing basis – Cystic Fibrosis.

In the 1960s, life expectancy of someone with CF was four years. It was considered a terminal disease. It is difficult to say how many died in those early years, because CF often went undiagnosed. In those days there was no screening for newborns, now widely available.

CF is an insidious genetic condition. A given gene, in my case the Delta 551 gene, is mutated. Extensive mischief and damage results. Specifically, mucus builds up in the lungs and causes repeated and constant infections. Over the years these infections wear away at the lungs until their function falls below 30% and a lung transplant becomes the only option.

The digestive system may also be affected: sticky mucous does not allow enzymes from the pancreas to do their work effectively: digesting fats and proteins. One of the first symptoms I experienced was a digestive issue at age 18 months. Despite a voracious appetite,

I was not thriving. CF was finally diagnosed when I was 2 ½ years old.

Stomach issues are part of CF for many, including me. Without the ability to properly digest food (even with the aid of digestive enzymes taken by capsule) my body does not absorb nutrients well. As a result, my body did not have the energy and resources to fight new infections. People with the disease may be prone to CF-related diabetes due to these pancreatic abnormalities.

The bravest sight in the world is to see a great man struggling against adversity.

SENECA

As I grew older and newer treatments were discovered, the life expectancy of someone with CF slowly and incrementally increased.

When I was six years old, life expectancy had increased to eight years of age.

When I was eight years old it was 12.

12 became 18.

18 became 28.

28 became 34.

And so on it went.

I am now 51, still just ahead of the CF life-expectancy curve defined by statisticians. While the statistics around life expectancy are and remain real I have always refused to allow a statistic to define what is possible. In fact, with new precision medication, CF is becoming a chronic condition and not a terminal one, and a cure is just around the corner. I fully intend my 80th birthday to be one for the history books.

> *Here is a rule to remember in future, when anything tempts you to feel bitter: not 'This is misfortune,' but 'To bear this worthily is good fortune.'*
>
> MARCUS AURELIUS

However the sad reality for too many CF patients is that the median age of death is 30 years of age. In Canada, we lose approximately 50 people a year to CF. Either they die or they receive a lung transplant. A transplant is substituting one terminal condition for another, as it merely buys time and is not a cure. The medications needed to fight the body's rejection of the transplanted organ are extensive, expensive, and onerous to administer.

In the pages that follow, I have set out a series of Life Lessons that have helped me to navigate the daily battle that a serious health condition presents. These principles have helped carry me through acute incidents that have resulted in various hospitalizations.

The lessons document the strategy, tactics, and attitudes that have allowed me to continuously stay ahead of the ominous curve imposed by CF. My hope is that whatever insights provided will help you, the reader, to overcome and outdistance your own health challenges, whatever they might be.

11 Lessons to Inform a Healthier and Happier Life

I try to live by the 11 lessons every day, in every way, to fight this silent but persistent foe. I offer them with the sincere belief that adoption of some or all of them to your own life will have a positive impact on your health and your life in general.

Of course, a healthcare crisis does not come when you are ready and prepared for it. The exact opposite is true. While we need sleep, infection never rests. It seems to strike when you are at your lowest ebb. It will come when you are least prepared to fight. Infections, whatever the underlying conditions, are always on their "A" game. They adapt, they mutate, they hunt and prey with the singular goal of wreaking havoc in your body. Viruses and infections are always around, even if we are able to fend them off for a time.

But when infection does strike (and it usually occurs when your body is in disarray), you are required to be at your best, under the circumstances, or at least rise to your best spiritual, mental, and physical self. You, however, are not prepared. It can feel like showing up to play in the Super Bowl when you have never been on a football team, or even touched a football, in your entire life. You've got 300-pound opposing players ready to pounce on you, and your goal is to get the ball into the end-zone.

As with the Super Bowl, everything is at stake. Unlike

the Super Bowl though, your team, (meaning *you*), have no experience at all. You are not playing a sport you're passionate about. Rather than being excited, you are wrought with fear, anxiety, and anger: all negative emotions you do *not* need if you are going to win.

Instead, you need to focus. Be consistent. Be disciplined. You need to own your attitude. It's the one and only thing that you have dominion over.

You find yourself in an environment entirely unfamiliar: a hospital. Death is lurking everywhere. Fear of dying is tangible from all sides.

The players on game day at the Super Bowl have prepared and practiced consistently and constantly for years leading up to that one game – training, practicing, and pushing their bodies to the breaking point to be ready to play, and to win.

You have done none of this. Even if you have a chronic condition from birth, like I do, a relapse always catches you when you are least ready for a fight. That's why it's a relapse.

What do you do? How do you make sure to leave vertically through the front door of the hospital, rather than being carried out horizontally through the back door?

The good news is everything I am suggesting requires no talent or hard lifting – though it does require practice! It is a matter of altering your perspective. Changing the way you view your world and your place in it.

A word that describes what underlies this attitude is resilience. When you cultivate your attitude, you sharpen and focus your resilience, a key ingredient to succeeding in this game called life.

As always, the simplest choices often have the greatest impact. The clearest and simplest choice you can make is how you shape your perspective. How do you choose to view the world around you? That simple choice will shape and determine so much of your life. It is a choice you are able to make, regardless of whether you are paralyzed from the neck down, or exhausted hiking up a hill.

The choice of how you view what confronts or befalls you: that is on you. Just as kindness is a choice and costs nothing, so too are attitude and perspective.

The choice is mandatory, if you want to survive a health crisis, to always focus on the stars. Focus on possibilities now, to prepare you for the next day.

There is not a soul on this planet who cannot execute a winning attitude. You need to start by coaching your perspective. As writer Jim Rohn reminds us: "Work harder on yourself than you do on your job."

It is easy to fall down or get off-track even when you have made a conscious decision to own your perspective. Don't fret. Simply hit re-focus and re-set when you find yourself going astray. I fall astray a dozen times a day. Sometimes a dozen times before breakfast!

The lessons outlined here will help. I can attest to

their simple transformative power on my perspective and view of life.

One of my favorite poems is "If –" by Rudyard Kipling. I always have it around.

If you can keep your head when all about you
Are losing theirs and blaming it on you;
If you can trust yourself when all men doubt you,
But make allowance for their doubting too;
If you can wait and not be tired by waiting,
Or being lied about, don't deal in lies,
Or being hated, don't give way to hating,
And yet don't look too good, nor talk too wise;

If you can dream—and not make dreams your master;
If you can think—and not make thoughts your aim,
If you can meet with Triumph and Disaster
And treat those two impostors just the same;
If you can bear to hear the truth you've spoken
Twisted by knaves to make a trap for fools,
Or watch the things you gave your life to, broken,
And stoop and build 'em up with worn-out tools;

If you can make one heap of all your winnings
And risk it on one turn of pitch-and-toss,
And lose, and start again at your beginnings
And never breathe a word about your loss;
If you can force your heart and nerve and sinew

To serve your turn long after they are gone,
And so hold on when there is nothing in you
Except the Will which says to them: "Hold on!"

If you can talk with crowds and keep your virtue,
Or walk with Kings—nor lose the common touch,
If neither foes nor loving friends can hurt you,
If all men count with you, but none too much;
If you can fill the unforgiving minute
With sixty seconds' worth of distance run,
Yours is the Earth and everything that's in it,
And—which is more—you'll be a Man, my son!

Always look for these kinds of inspirations. They come in all forms and through many different voices, as will be evident in the pages that follow.

LESSON 1

Attitude is Everything

"To overcome fear, the best thing is to be overwhelmingly grateful."
SIR JOHN TEMPLETON

The first lesson that I adopted was: if you think you're sick, or if you think you're healthy, you're right.

Mind-set matters. A lot. You need to work on it constantly, every day in ways small and large … but mostly small.

Life chips away at even the best attitude. Steel yourself against the small, insidious comments or attitudes of others. In today's world it is actually cool to be cynical. It means you are sophisticated. Being thoughtful, as in one who thinks deeply, means that you don't buy into the system. You think critically. Positive thinking is looked down on in many circles. People think that it takes away from the real and serious systemic problems in the world.

is the reality: you can fully acknowledge the ... challenges of poverty, disease and inequality, and still have a positive attitude.

Do not indulge in dreams of having what you have not, but reckon up the chief of the blessings you do possess, and then thankfully remember how you would crave for them if they were not yours.
MARCUS AURELIUS

Remember that each day is another chance and choice to impact one life. That life is your own. It is the one that you are completely responsible for. How I lead my life and what I do with it has a ripple effect on the world around me. It is with my response, such as it is, to everything around me that I can choose to change the world, and first by changing my perception of the world.

Rosa Parks created a tidal wave of change because she was sick and tired. Not of standing. Sick and tired of giving in. She resolved not to give in that day. She made a choice, took a chance, to make a change. That is what happens when you decide to change something in your life. You control your response, including the attitude you adopt. That decision makes all the difference. The Montgomery bus boycotts ensued and Dr. Martin Luther King Jr. took centre stage in America and indeed the world.

The best approach to life is to choose an attitude of gratitude. Always be grateful to be alive in this game called life.

Our mind can only hold one overarching concept at a time. You cannot be angry and grateful at the same time. If you are grateful, you can't be fearful. Choose to be grateful. It will sustain you when all else fails you. Gratitude is an all-encompassing emotion. When you're grateful there is room for no other emotions.

Very little is needed to make a happy life; it is all within yourself, in your way of thinking.
MARCUS AURELIUS

An attitude of gratitude along with the force of sheer will reshapes everything. You need to be grateful for what you have, starting with the simple fact that you are alive and in the fight. At the start of every day write down three things that you are grateful for.

14 June 2012. I was admitted to St. Michael's Hospital in Toronto, which is known as "Canada's Urban Angel." This particular time in the hospital was a long and challenging trek. I had a short remission, but was back again in August, and stayed there until November.

The stay was perilous.

My struggle was to elevate my lung function score above 30% FEV1. (That is, Forced Expiratory Volume in 1 second). At this level you either raise the numbers, or you get in line for a lung transplant, an option of last resort.

During that dark time at St. Mike's my medical team used many antibiotics, but to no avail. The treatment regime included rigorous physiotherapy, lung clearance, nutrition, and whatever exercise I could muster. The latter was primarily doing laps late into the night around the 6th floor of the building … with an oxygen tank in tow as I needed all the supplemental oxygen it could offer.

I won't soon forget the first day I woke up in that room on ward 6B. I wrote down three things I was grateful for:

- A room with a view: my window overlooked a church. I saw rays of sunshine, light.
- Rising sun. A new day is a fresh shot at life. A clear reminder I'm still in the game.
- Ability to still walk for coffee every morning … that first coffee of the day from the shop across the street.

It took every ounce of energy I had to make my walk across the street. I had to disconnect from the IV pole, put a knob lock in the IV stem in my arm, and then take off the supplemental oxygen (4 litres a minute) and then proceed with oxygen levels falling dangerously close to 90 … rapidly. I had an Oxygen reader to keep track while I shuffled … paused, leaned on whatever was near me and continued down the elevator, out the door and across the street. The most trying part was steps or inclines. I did everything I could to avoid any elevation.

You gain tremendous perspective on what a real challenge in life is when simply walking and breathing become such incredible ordeals.

My shuffle had no sense of a stride.

It filled me with awe – at how incredibly blessed anyone is who has the ability to breathe and walk with ease. Every one of us takes it for granted. (I take it for granted once again, now that I am back in the game of life.)

During that period at St. Mike's it was so easy to find things to be grateful for because the commonplace became extraordinarily difficult. I was up and looking out that window every morning with gratitude for what I had. That empowered my day. It was as important to me as food, water, and medicine.

The medicine wasn't working. I knew I was ill. Too ill. I was not recovering. But I never lost hope. I received a trilogy of blessings daily: Faith, Hope, Love.

Faith in God. A hope that tomorrow will in fact truly be better than today. Love from the most unlikely of sources: porters, nurses, staff, orderlies, the people in the beds next to me, and their visitors. And, of course, my own family and friends who were amazing. They were supportive beyond words. I was particularly struck by the kindness of strangers. My stay was akin to spending five months on the road to Jericho.

From three very different and diverse thinkers I draw my understanding of gratitude and the overwhelmingly important place and role it must have if you are to succeed in a health crisis:

- Brother David Steindl-Rast, a Benedictine monk. He has reached millions with his TED Talk on gratitude as the key to happiness.

He focuses on the reality that true happiness comes from valuing each moment as a gift. Every moment is a fresh opportunity, whatever it may bring. Yet another opportunity to be grateful.

One consistent reality is that as long as you are alive you have the next moment, and the next, and the next. Each, another opportunity in life. There are always more opportunities.

Brother David suggests using the tactic of stop/look/go. Stop to realize and recognize the opportunities in a given moment. Look and be aware of what that is. Then go and seize the moment, filled with gratitude that it is yours.

Stop to realize you're alive and can be grateful. Look at what you have received and then go seize the day.

- Brother John Main, another Benedictine monk. He re-introduced the power of meditation from the desert fathers in the Christian/Catholic tradition. I have gained much by focusing on his teachings of meditative practice and integrating it with the art of being grateful.

- An American motivator who appreciates that the art of fulfillment is essential to your well-being: Tony Robbins, one of the gurus of teaching control of your response to your circumstance.

In his book *Unshakeable* Tony directly addresses the question of happiness and how to master what he calls the art of fulfillment. It provides some tools and tactics, and illustrates the need for gratitude every day.

As Tony says: It is essential that you start each day by writing down three things you are grateful for. If you don't have pen or paper, or cannot write because you're too damn sick, then reflect on what you are grateful for.

Every time you feel yourself being overcome by feelings or emotions that cloud your thoughts, follow the 90-second rule: reflect for 90 seconds on something you are grateful for. It is not hard. The mere fact that you are alive, have a brain to reflect and think, and a heart that beats, is pretty much a lottery-winning place to start.

Everyone on earth has seen hardship and pain. Everyone at some point asks the ultimate question, which has been known throughout the ages as the theodicy question: "Why do bad things happen to good people?"

Rabbi Harold Kushner grappled with this when his

son died at the age of 12. He took a hard look at the Book of Job and penned some profound observations and considerations.

As is a tale, so is life: not how long it is, but how good it is, is what matters.
SENECA

I have no idea why bad things happen to good people, but I can give two examples.

I knew a young boy named Courtney during my years growing up in Saskatoon. I did not know him well. He and I would always meet at gatherings of CF families, particularly fundraising events to raise money to find a cure for CF.

We were 10 years apart. I was 18 and he was eight when we met. His image always stuck with me. He was always smiling and laughing and filled with life and fight. CF hit him particularly hard.

I knew him well enough to know that attitude and a fight for life were his in abundance. He exuded a winning attitude – the attitude that I describe in this book was his in spades.

Perhaps what struck me most was the contrast. Why and how was it that I went into the same hospital as he did and had the same condition he had, he passed and I didn't?

He and I shared the same attitude. In fact, I learned a lot about having a winning attitude from him. When an eight year old has wisdom through experience, and a smile and a spark in his eye that comes from challenging times, so much can be learned from even brief encounters with these remarkable souls. I learned immeasurable amounts from my brief encounters with Courtney.

Despite that attitude, and a wisdom uncommon for an eight year old, he was taken far too young. It shook me because it ran contrary to all I believed about attitude and bringing fight to the game.

Think of yourself as dead. You have lived your life. Now take what's left and live it properly.
MARCUS AURELIUS

It's a reminder that is scarred into my consciousness. Even attitude needs allies to win the fight. It's sometimes all we can bring, but on its own, it's not necessarily enough.

Courtney lived a life fully, and with mental fortitude and true resilience. A tremendous young kid, Courtney was a great example of the ultimate winning attitude. You could ask for no more "give" and "win" than this young guy had.

Courtney had CF, entirely not of his making. When someone so young succumbs to a genetic disease, I can only assume all the angels in heaven take a moment to pause. When any child dies, there is no explanation and only a feeling of overwhelming sadness.

I tell this story because I am talking about mindset. We can bring the best attitude to every day and every game. We can say emphatically: "It's on me and it is my attitude that can save the day." Attitude remains the only thing that you can bring to the game. The imprint Courtney left on my life stays with me.

I can only describe his death as an absolutely jaw-dropping shocker. How can somebody with his courageous attitude and his will to live be taken so young? It is a direct challenge to everything I speak about and ask you to focus on in the lessons to follow. Courtney also left us an amazing gift — the memory of his time with us.

I love the concept that you die twice: once when you pass away, and a second time when the last person with memories of you dies.

This underscores the import of the impression we leave on others, both positive and negative. Knowing that what you do has a significant and lasting impact, it is vital to try to do all the good you can all the time you can, in any way you can. As John Wesley counseled:

"Do all the good you can,
By all the means you can,
In all the ways you can,
In all the places you can,
At all the times you can,
To all the people you can,
As long as ever you can."

The life Courtney lived, with the attitude he exhibited, was exactly the mark each of us must strive to leave on everyone around us.

Another life lost all too soon from CF was Ron, a true icon in my mind. He was in his early 30s when I met him. He came to Saskatoon where he was a keynote speaker at a CF fundraiser. He was invited to speak on his amazing story of running an ironman triathalon. He had two children. He ran a vibrant small business, a cycling store in Edmonton. Most astonishing from my perspective is that his attitude won the day. He did the impossible. I first heard about Ron by word of mouth and decided to call him prior to ever meeting him. I tracked down his number (this was in 1991 so well before the internet!). He described to me over the phone his story and how he managed to run the ironman against all odds.

> *Death smiles at us all, but all a man can do is smile back.*
>
> MARCUS AURELIUS

He began training for, and ultimately ran, cycled, and swam the grueling Penticton Ironman: a 160-mile bike ride, a 6-mile swim, and a 26-mile marathon. Penticton is known as one of the world's premier triathlon host communities.

Ron did this when anyone else in their 30s, with the condition he had, would be dead. I was in a state of shock and awe. What would be a challenge by any standard, for a person with CF becomes a miracle writ large. He epitomized resilience.

He taught me that absolutely anything is possible. Mind wins over matter.

I almost had a heart attack when I heard the news of his passing in 2012. He was taken much too early. It wasn't until eight years later that I Googled him to find out what happened. I did not want to know. I prayed that it had nothing to do with CF and that it was some sort of accident. I never found out, and I still have no idea how he passed. But I am sure of one thing. The fight he waged was certainly the stuff legends are made of, and his memory continues to inspire me today.

In my life I still use his example as a reference point when anything seems impossible. We lost Ron, but Ron won. In this life, he beat CF and proved the impossible can be done.

There truly are no limits to what the mind can achieve when in a state of flow, and the mindset is right.

Each of us has the personal challenge to focus and work as hard on our own attitude as we do on anything else. It is not an occasional effort. It must be done with intention at the start of each day, and constantly throughout.

We must catch ourselves when the world collides with us. Refocus and commit once again to owning our attitude, even when the reality of the world and all common sense would dictate that only a fool would be optimistic.

It is exactly when only a fool would see the situation as an opportunity that you need to have the mindset of Courtney and Ron.

LESSON NOTES

Attitude is Everything

LESSON 2

Be the CEO of Your Own Health

You cannot be dependent on others. You need to take ultimate responsibility for your life and your health.

In his book *Extreme Ownership* Jocko Willink talks about this. To summarize the essence of what he says: As a commander of the Navy Seals, whatever the situation of those whose life he was responsible for, he owned. Even if it was not of his making. He never asked for special accommodation. Whenever he did ask a commanding officer for additional supplies, he got it. They knew he only asked when it was a critical situation. There was no complaint from his platoon.

I do not recall when I first realized this, but it was clear that the only way forward for me was to take full responsibility for the good, the bad, and the ugly in my life, since no one else would or could.

It is all too easy to blame chance, bad luck, parents, family, culture, or your community for your circumstance. I don't know why bad things happen to good people, but they do. The only answer I can come up with is that you may have been dealt a bad hand of cards. But as with anything in life, the joy is turning whatever hand you've been dealt into a winning play.

Great stories come as a result of a bad hand dealt to a person who then comes out on top. If you are alive, if you're breathing, there is no bad hand – there is simply the hand you've been dealt.

You are the boss of your own health. You need to learn leadership skills. You need to rally the troops. You need to keep your spirits high. You need to keep your focus sharp.

Regardless of what you do in life – if you're a student or employed or looking for work or unable to work – during a health crisis you are immediately elevated to the role of Chief Executive Officer, the CEO, of your own health. You have a team that you need to lead, motivate and inspire. Ultimately, the buck stops with you. And you have been designated as the CEO of your own health enterprise.

You are the minister of health, premier, prime minister, president, and the head of state, coach, and captain all rolled into one. The doctors, the nurses, the physiotherapists, the technicians – they are all members of your team.

You need to take what they say as counsel, but ultimately you make the decision. When making a decision, always choose life.

In my experience, there are many examples of why

you need to own the situation, your own decisions, and not simply let others do so for you.

Camp Easter Seal

When I was a kid, there were two summer camps near Saskatoon. The one run by the YMCA was for healthy kids. The Easter Seal Camp was for children with disabilities, and children with diabetes – and then came the year they decided to include children with CF.

I respect anyone with a disability, but I did not want to be sent to a camp for kids with disabilities. Who wants to be sent to a camp because of one's health? It was done with good intentions, but in my view this was simply bad policy.

> *Caretake this moment. Immerse yourself in its particulars. Respond to this person, this challenge, this deed. Quit evasions. Stop giving yourself needless trouble. It is time to really live; to fully inhabit the situation you happen to be in now.*
>
> EPICTETUS

CF Camp

The following year I went to a summer camp for kids with CF only. In theory, this is a neat idea. I met others with CF and it was a lot of fun and you could share experiences.

People with CF are vulnerable to different bacteria and bugs, which grow in their lungs. While these bugs are harmless to people who don't have CF, they can settle in and colonize the lungs and be harmful for those who do. These bugs can be easily transmitted from one CF person to another. The place had the potential to turn into camps with deadly consequences. In retrospect, it was a well-intentioned but bad policy.

> *Man is affected not by events, but by the view he takes of them.*
> SENECA

Group Sessions for Physiotherapy

We used to go into hospital for physiotherapy. CF patients beside CF patients, COPD patients, and anyone else that required daily physiotherapy.

At the time it was fun because we ended up having lots of great discussions. Today you would never have multiple CF patients in a room for physiotherapy.

CF Clinics Now Require Patients 6 Feet Apart At All Times

In fact, CF clinics now require patients to wear masks when they arrive and ensure that all patients stay at least six feet apart. This is still a relatively new precaution, implemented years before COVID-19 mask and social distancing requirements. However, for the first 35 years I was a patient at CF clinics there was no six-foot rule.

These are examples of policy choices made by smart, capable people — policy choices that turned out to be deadly. It was no one's fault, and fault ought not to be allocated. But it's a reminder that just because someone suggests something, that doesn't make it a good idea or the right thing to do.

As the CEO of your health, take the lead. Be the leader of the team. If the nurse comes to take your blood, ask what tests are getting done and why; then follow-up on the results. Always ask your doctors how they're doing. Check up on them and be there for them. This includes every member of your medical team.

Make sure everything around you is signed off by you. It is far too easy just to sit or lie there as a patient and simply be given prognoses and programs for recovery, acting like a bystander to what happens to you.

Sometimes you may make bad choices. Here are two questionable choices I've made.

One clearly wrong choice was in the early years, when I refused to go to the hospital. I simply would not go. I'm sure one of the reasons why my lung function is 50% instead of 70% is because I refused to be an in-patient in the early years, thus not adequately addressing the regular infections that occurred.

No one wears that one but me. I ultimately did go to the hospital when a doctor said to me: "If you don't go, you'll be dead."

The reason I was so reticent was because everyone I've ever seen that went in ultimately died, all far too young. They went to get treated and it just never ended.

They went the first time, and then the next, and every time they got sick they were hospitalized and were told they needed IV antibiotics.

Sometimes even to live is an act of courage.
SENECA

These friends would tell me what they were being told by the doctors, and none of it was any good. I wanted nothing to do with it.

Before it became medically necessary to keep CF patients six feet apart and not socialize, we often socialized together. I used to visit my very dear friend Jessica when she was sick and was in hospital.

It was terrible. She was very ill. She couldn't breathe. The rooms were dark and unpleasant.

In my opinion, institutionalization kills more people than illness does. You need to fight it as hard as you fight the health condition. What I mean by this is that it is so very easy to become comfortable and complacent in the hospital setting. The comfort that comes from being cared for, looked after by an army of individuals, including orderlies, porters, nurses, cooks, and cleaning staff. Even if you want to, they will not let you walk to get an X-ray on another floor of the hospital. A porter will come for you and he will either wheel your bed or put you in a wheelchair and take you there.

You then wait to be picked up from that test and returned to your room. While in your room, if you require anything, whether it be as simple as a glass of water or an extra blanket you just press a button and someone will attend to you.

There is no self-help allowed. I understand the policy reasons that underscore this (a sick patient trips or falls, or gets lost and misses an appointment, and the hospital could be liable). Frankly, most people that are in hospital are too sick to move. But with a condition like CF, patients are often not completely immobilized. They can generally move around. They end up for weeks and weeks in the hospital environment, as slow-drip intravenous antibiotics are the primary way to fight infection.

In my experience, it is the weeks in this environment that are dangerous for the psyche. They steal a person's independence.

It is critical to guard against this loss of independence with every fibre of your being. When I speak of institutionalization it's this mischief that I am referring to. The loss of independence and becoming wholly dependent on others to care for your most basic needs.

Early on, what I perceived as Jessica's experience with hospitals and treatment made me never want to go into a hospital, ever.

Jessica also passed far too young. It was tragic, as it is every time someone dies before their time.

But let's be clear: if your medical team recommends that you come into hospital to treat an acute infection, you must go. There is no question. My remarks address the awareness I believe everyone needs to have of the challenge imposed by allowing for an emotional dependency within the hospital environment. I say this as one who has fallen prey to it. I have seen others close to me fall victim to it, and it must be guarded against constantly.

The impediment to action advances action. What stands in the way becomes the way.
MARCUS AURELIUS

The other likely wrong decision I made was when I refused to get a PICC line: a peripherally inserted central catheter. The catheter is inserted into an artery. It makes life easier for patient and doctor. It can last up to three months and doesn't require constant changes to the site. It also allows for fast and efficient delivery of medications and taking of blood. In contrast, an IV is inserted into the lower arm and lasts for only a few days before the site needs to be changed due to irritation and inflammation.

In my mind I did not like the long-term nature of the PICC line. It had a sense of permanence that cried out "institutionalization" in my mind.

Refusing to get a PICC line afforded me a decision I could make that went against the grain. It allowed me to take a small measure of control that stood in complete contrast to what everyone else was doing and was recommended by healthcare providers.

My friend Jessica, who I spoke of earlier, introduced me to the reality of a PICC line. She told me they used a PICC line in her case because she was spending so much time in the hospital, that it just made life easier.

Her words at the time, and even now, ring loudly in my ear. They haunted me then and they still haunt me.

I promised myself I would never do anything to make my life easier in a hospital setting.

I wanted to constantly be reminded that if a hospital stay was necessary, I would do nothing to make it pleasant or easy to bear. I needed it to be a combat zone and a mighty struggle as a mechanism to fend off the institutionalization I was equally terrified of setting in.

Clearly I was wrong. It is a simple medical procedure and tool to help make the life of patients and staff easier and more efficient.

Another example of me making a decision that I am accountable for.

During my last stay in 2018 at the age of 48, I relented and requested a PICC line when I was taking an antibiotic regime that included Cipro and Piperacillin. For whatever reason, the combination of these medications or the irritation caused in my veins … I could literally feel the drugs course through my veins, through my entire body. It was excruciating.

I finally told my doctor that I couldn't take the pain any longer.

After it had been going on for a few days I was ready for the PICC line — anything to reduce the pain. Fortunately, my doctor said it would take three days before I could get one inserted and I was to be out of the hospital in two days. To this day I have avoided a PICC line.

I am now on Kalydeco and a hospital stay is not a death sentence. Finally, I am prepared to have a PICC line.

I tell these stories because every decision made is a choice we own, period. I own every decision I've made, even when I didn't necessarily make it.

That is what it means to be the CEO of your own health. At one point I was labeled a difficult patient. I was told I was in denial. That may well have been the case.

You Need to Be An Advocate for Yourself

Another, and final, example of insisting on being the CEO of your own health is that you need to be an advocate. At whatever level it is, a patient needs to be an extraordinary advocate for their own well-being.

First, an instance where I failed to be my own advocate.

I found myself sitting and waiting for help in a hospital. Recall, I am a lawyer by trade. I had these advocacy principles engrained in my head. Despite my profession, I found myself waiting for my doctor to tell me whether I would get a life-saving medication or not. Day after day went by. I sat there, waiting to hear the result.

It started on Monday, 22 September 2012 (with my lung function at less than 30%). My doctor, Elizabeth Tullis, the leading CF doctor in Canada and a leading respirologist in the world, came into my shared room.

She said, "Chris, I have good news and bad news."

I told her: "We have a moratorium on bad news. Good news only!"

Her response: "You have a rare form of CF. You have the Delta 551 gene type. There is a company, Vertex Pharmaceuticals in Boston, that has developed a treatment and resulting medication that will normalize this gene defect. The challenge: it has only been approved by the FDA in the United States and has not yet been submitted to Canada, and it's costly."

The drug was called Kalydeco, the first gene modulator that normalizes the gene defect in certain mutations of the CF gene – mine included.

Dr. Tullis then went on with the bad news: "You are very sick. Our only recourse at this point is to look at pre-transplant review and ultimately place you on a lung transplant list."

Fortunately, Vertex Pharmaceuticals has a compassionate use program, as do most pharma companies. They agreed to provide me with the medicine without charge.

But there was a hitch. Because the medicine did not have approval from the federal Ministry of Health it could not even enter the country without approval from the Special Access Program. This program would allow medication not approved by the federal government into the country at the request of a doctor if:

- the need was urgent and the situation life threatening
- the drug was needed for a temporary use
- there were no other available options in the market.

The typical response time for approval of a medication under these urgent circumstances from the federal government is 24 hours. This underscored the urgency.

However, *in my case* with the application for Special Access to Kalydeco there simply was no response. Not a yes, or even a no. Simply no response.

I proceeded to follow-up with Dr. Tullis's office day after day for the remainder of that week. I finally realized I needed to stop asking others to do this for me and I had to figure out what was going on. I had to roll up my sleeves, work with my team, and get it done.

Yet, even in this situation, in contrast to the very philosophy I'm championing in this book, I found myself sitting and waiting for something to be done for me.

I decided that I had to figure out how to get access to this drug. I told my good friend Doug about the pickle I was in. He said that for the first time ever he heard fear in my voice.

He then proceeded to do a full forensic analysis on the special access program. He quarterbacked all communication, including the emails sent when we went to war with the federal government for access to this life-sustaining medication.

The pressure was on. The only other option was a lung transplant, heading into flu season … It was not looking good.

It matters not how strait the gate,
How charged with punishment the scroll,
I am the master of my fate : I am the captain of my soul.

"INVICTUS" BY WILLIAM ERNEST HENLEY

As the rapper Eminem said: "Success is my only motherfuckin' option—failure's not."

Despite weeks and weeks of a 24/7 slow-drip, and fast-drip multiple drug combinations delivered intravenously, rigorous physiotherapy, eating six times daily, my weight continued to fall below 150 pounds. I simply could not move the dial and improve my situation.

Also, the hospital bed was needed for others, and the concern that I was simply going to continue to get worse and risk getting sicker with added infections if I stayed in the hospital.

We decided to keep me in for another two weeks and see what we could do to get access to the medication.

The Advocacy Campaign for Access to Kalydeco

I've always been politically engaged. I've been blessed not with financial resources but with legions of friends: brothers and sisters, all whom have always been at-the-ready to care for my interest, as I will and have always cared for theirs.

Thirty-five different individuals — a former premier, cabinet ministers, senators, journalists, members of parliament, members of the provincial parliament, and many others, old friends and new, and complete strangers who were simply just great Canadians — came to bat for me.

They moved heaven and earth for the kid from Saskatchewan.

This incredible crew ultimately forced the federal Minister of Health, the Honorable Leona Aglukkaq, to intervene and to override the bad bureaucratic decision to deny my special access application (despite the fact that government was not paying a penny for my treatment).

I will always remember the last conversation I had with my medical team. The drug had not yet arrived.

"Chris, we need the bed. There's absolutely nothing these antibiotics are doing for you. The medication you need is Kalydeco. It's your last best hope, not the bed in this hospital."

Ultimately the right thing was done. I was given access to the medication.

Within 10 days of commencing the treatment, on 30 November 2012, my lung function climbed from 30% to over 50%.

Having had so many people do so much to secure access for me, I was beholden to secure access for others. As a direct result of our efforts to secure access for me to Kalydeco, four others were given immediate access to the drug, alongside me.

I admit that, at the time, I had no concept that to secure access to gene modulators for others was actually going to be such a long and difficult road.

I decided to call the then-Assistant Deputy Minister of Health of Ontario, who manages the drug file. I wanted to relay the anecdote of the success of this medication on my health and to inform the ADM that as a citizen it was my recommendation to her to list this drug on the provincial formulary.

I thought that the simple fact that I was making the call and relaying an important healthcare success story would be sufficient to expedite the process of securing access for those without a Group Benefit Plan (i.e. private drug coverage).

As it turns out, it was anything but a straightforward process.

I was told the ADM did not meet with individuals. That led me to establish the Canadian Cystic Fibrosis Treatment Society in order to attempt to secure a meeting and to advocate for individuals that need access to medicines like Kalydeco. I will leave the rest of this story for another day.

Suffice to say, it has been an eight-year campaign that has taken the time and energy of so many individuals — energy and time that could have been spent doing other work such as creating jobs and opportunities for individuals.

Instead, all too much human capital and time – tens of thousands of hours – have been spent fighting our own government to facilitate access for those few that do not have a Group Benefit Plan and need a hand-up. This represents a true loss in the opportunity cost column of our nation's human resources.

This time in my life solidified my firm belief in extreme ownership. If you ever find yourself a patient in a hospital or the healthcare system, you must act like the CEO of your own healthcare plan. Lead, manage, motivate, and advocate. Make the decisions and live with the consequences.

With extreme ownership comes extreme responsibility. Not only do you need to advocate for yourself but if you've been blessed with the position, place, and privilege where you can get life-sustaining access to medications and healthcare in a society that looks after the most vulnerable (as it should be) you then have a co-equal responsibility to move heaven and earth so that no one is left behind.

LESSON NOTES

Be the CEO of Your Own Health

Chris as a 3 month old baby in Montreal.

Chris at the age of 12 months in Saskatoon.

Chris in Saskatoon at the age of 2 years.

Chris in Saskatoon at the age of 3 years.

Chris at his grandfather's farm in Hamiota, Manitoba at the age of 8 years with one of his grandfather Hudson's horses.

Chris with Ron Moore in Saskatoon, approximately 1990.

Graduation from Law School, University of Saskatchewan in the year 2000.

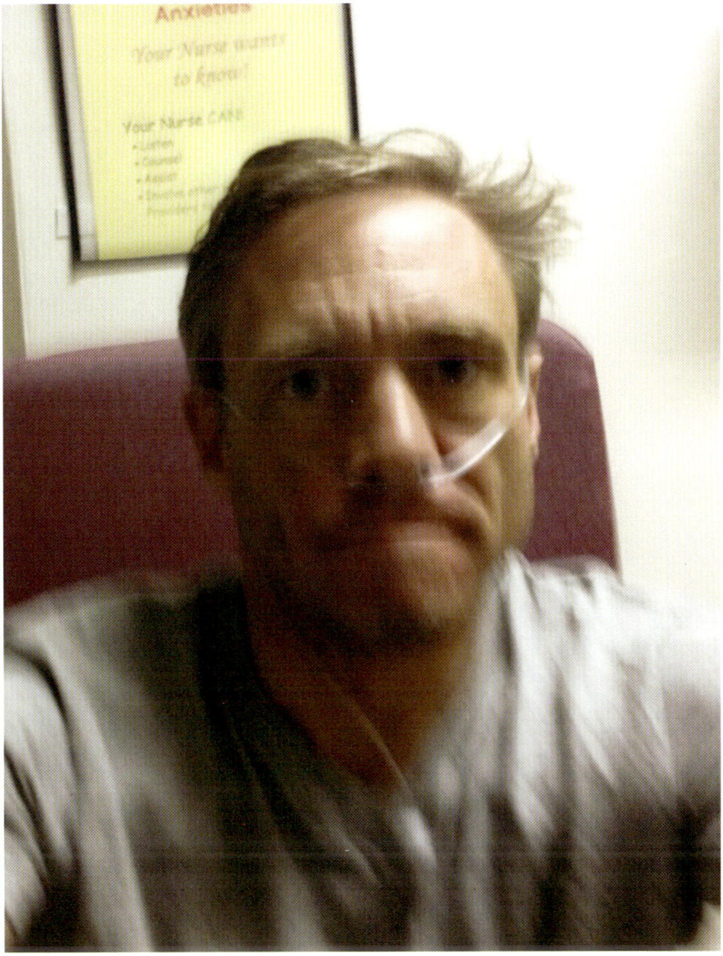

Chris in St. Michael's Hospital (Toronto) in 2012 on 4 litres of oxygen a minute, less than 30% lung function.

The white board that hung in Chris's room at St. Michael's Hospital (Toronto) where he wrote out his goals... 65% lung function and a weight of 165 pounds.

St. Michael's Hospital Pulmonary Function / Trend Report

Name: MACLEOD, CHRISTOPHER
Age: 43
Sex : Male
Height : 69.3 in / 176 cm
Weight : 166 lb / 75.4 kg

Id: J2540481
Encounter # 524368909
Hb: gm/dl
BMI: 24.34

Date: 06/25/2013 (MM/DD/YR)
Smoker: No Quit: No
Pack Years:
RFR: CF
Physician: Elizabeth Tullis
Tested by: EL 6

PulAcct|524368909|Full PFT Report DOT: 06/25/2013

		Ref	Lower-Upper Limit	Pre	% Ref	Post	% Ref	%Chg
Spirometry								
FVC	Liters	5.24	(4.3 - 6.2)	** 3.78	** 72			
FEV1	Liters	4.15	(3.3 - 5.0)	** 2.34	** 56			
FEV1/FVC	%	80	(70.9 - 90.1)	** 62	** 77			
FEF50%	L/sec	4.77	LLN: M-61%, F-65%	1.93	41			
FEF75%	L/sec	1.71	LLN: M-55%, F-65%	0.40	23			

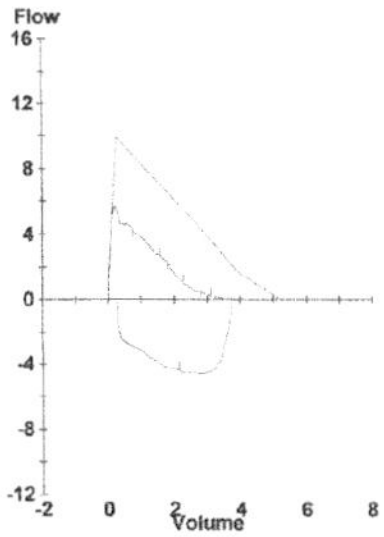

**(Outside of 90% Confidence Interval)

Technologist's Comments: Lower-Upper Limit for Raw: 66%-177%
SpO2 96%, HR 81 bpm on room air. Spirometry data acceptable & reproducible.

Previous Study:04/02/2013		Current Study:06/25/2013			
FVC	3.40 Liters	FVC	3.78 Liters	(72) %	improved by 11%
FEV1	2.11 Liters	FEV1	2.34 Liters	(56) %	improved by 11%
VC	Liters	VC	Liters	() %	improved by
TLC	Liters	TLC	Liters	() %	improved by
RV	Liters	RV	Liters	() %	improved by
DLCO	mL/mmHg/min	DLCO	mL/mmHg/min	() %	improved by
VA	Liters	VA	Liters	() %	improved by

Date	FVC	FEV1	VC	PEF	TLC	RV	DLCO
06/25/2013	3.78 (L)	2.34 (L)	(L)	6.29 (L/S)	(L)	(L)	(ml/mmHg/min)
04/02/2013	3.40	2.11		5.61			
01/15/2013	3.24	2.08		5.79			
11/27/2012	3.26	1.94		6.27			
10/31/2012	2.70	, 1.48	2.70	5.14	6.29	3.59	21.6

The pulmonary function test results before and after Chris starts the medication Kalydeco.

Chris speaking at a CF fundraiser in 2018 and telling his story of Beating the Odds.

LESSON 3

There is Power in Your Response

You cannot control what happens to you but you do have dominion over your response to it. Make your response bold, positive and daring!

As I said earlier, I have no idea why bad things happen to good people. Sometimes shit just happens. Regardless of the cards you're dealt in life, the one and only one thing that you have complete control over is your response.

With a hospital stay or a healthcare crisis, the reality is that it happened. It is what it is. You cannot turn it back. Here are some strategies to use:

- This is a war. You are officially in battle mode.
- Treat it like the Super Bowl or a military campaign.
- Respond with gratitude.
- Always be hopeful.
- Have faith that "this too shall pass."

My first *significant* hospitalization occurred in the late 1990s. Prior to this an infection could be treated with intravenous antibiotics over ten days or two weeks. In those previous incidents of hospitalization, the infection was manageable.

In the fall of 1997, I had my first confrontation with an infection that almost got the best of me – one that required me to implement the lessons in this book, particularly in this chapter, with absolute clarity. The prospects were bleak and the risk that I might not come out of it were very real.

I had been accepted to law school. I was returning home to Saskatoon. My first few weeks of school, starting in September, were terrific. However, infection is insidious. It creeps up on you.

It did, in a dramatic way, that first semester.

Few things are more troubling or disconcerting than bleeding internally, particularly when the bleed is in your lungs.

It's not so much pain that you feel. It is a sense of weakness, of helplessness, that comes over you. You hear a gurgling sound. There is so much blood in your lungs that it's coming up through your throat. You are coughing up blood to try to rid yourself of it.

In my case, it was also coming out my nose. I thought I had a nose bleed. My immediate reaction was that the blood in my throat was a result of the nose bleed.

It proved not to be a nose bleed but a severe case of hemoptysis. Coughing up blood. My nose was not bleeding … it was just a funnel to rid the body of blood in my lungs.

It's scary because you can't control it. There is very little you can do. You cannot will it to stop. You can only control your response to it. The actions you choose to take or not to take. The mind set you bring to bear on the crisis before you.

The first reaction is terrifying fear, particularly when it happens for the first time. I had coughed up blood prior to this, but I had never experienced this free flow of blood from my nose and throat.

I went to the emergency room and was promptly admitted. I spent the better part of the next several weeks at the hospital. Considering the first semester only has about 12 weeks this put me up against the wall.

First year and first semester are an intense period in law school. It's also all new. There are few, if any, papers or assignments. It all comes down to 100% final exams written in December.

I was fortunate because the Royal University Hospital where I was admitted is actually on campus. It's a teaching hospital about 500 meters from the law school.

My response to the illness and infection was only a small part of what I needed to deal with. As important was my response to life, to all the other activities of my life.

Everything I do, or anyone does, is a choice and a response to the present environment and the current situation. I made the decision that my response to the infection and the massive bleed would be that nothing – and everything – would change.

I met with the medical team. I told them I would do whatever they recommended I do to treat this infection, with one important caveat. I decided that if the infection took me down, then I would fall fully engaged in the activity of living.

I would not miss a class or delay an examination. I would not quit, drop out, or miss a beat of the workload I had.

I am sure if I had asked to put off the semester until this situation had passed, no one would have said anything other than they understood and wished me well for a speedy recovery. But that would be giving a win to an illness that I was not prepared to give a win to.

I was told by numerous people, including doctors and nurses, that my illness would be aggravated if I carried on with my activities instead of simply resting. They were likely right. But for me, I had control over only one thing: my response to this situation.

I couldn't stop the bleed, and the infection would subside with rest, but I could neither rest nor work with either one holding exclusive power over my life.

I believed then, as I still do now, that to focus on something other than your illness is the only way to beat the illness. You need to relegate it to the sidelines of your life. It helps to have so much before you that you seek to accomplish that the illness becomes a nuisance to be tended to and not a preoccupation.

> *You don't have to turn this into something. It doesn't have to upset you.*
> MARCUS AURELIUS

First I had to survive and come out alive, which meant the bleeding needed to stop. Clearly there would be damage to the lungs, but the bleeding needed to end.

Intravenous antibiotics were administered. They just were not doing the trick. The medication was taking too long to strike a blow at the infection. The resultant bleeding came when I least expected it or wanted it.

The choices I had to impact the bleeding were few. I could take the intravenous antibiotics, rest to heal, exercise and clear my lungs as best I could without agitating further bleeds.

Intravenous antibiotics are administered every six hours (in this instance) so there is space and time to get work done in the intervening period. I didn't feel so ill that I couldn't walk or talk. I managed the intravenous treatments around classes to the best of my ability.

Class was not physically strenuous as I was sitting and when I didn't move the bleeding was lessened or paused. But I did keep a "traveller mug" to be sure I had somewhere to spit in the event of a bleed.

I spent more time in class praying not to bleed than answering any questions.

I was hired for $100 a meeting (if I recall the amount correctly) to chair the USSU (University of Saskatchewan Student Union) council meetings once a month, so I attended the meetings with an IV in my arm, but knob-locked for my mobility.

While I was ultimately discharged from the hospital and passed that first semester, the bleeding persisted and remained a challenge for the next two years in law school.

The recommendation by the doctors was to stay put in Saskatchewan and not travel out of province, and certainly not by plane.

However, life doesn't stop for anyone or anything. While it presents challenges it also provides opportunities.

In my second year of law school, while grounded from travel, I received news that I was a finalist in an essay contest sponsored by the industrialist and famed entrepreneur, the legendary Frank Stronach.

Frank's story is incredible. He came to Canada in 1954 with 20 dollars in his pocket as a tool and die maker from Austria. He set up a shop to make auto parts and eventually became the world's largest auto parts maker, employing 178,000 people in 450 factories in 38 countries.

Frank is an idea generator. He is also committed to Canada. In 1995, the nation had just gone through a constitutional crisis, resulting in the Quebec referendum to determine if Quebec should separate from Canada.

The "No" side won … by a hair. Frank decided to put together an essay contest and asked young Canadians what they recommend to unite the country and improve the economy. Thousands of students from across the country wrote a 1,500 word essay entitled "If I were Prime Minister I would …"

I decided to put pen to paper and submit an essay.

Ten essay writers were selected as finalists. In the late summer of 1998 we were all flown to Toronto to be interviewed by a panel of judges. Then in the fall there was a return flight for the ten finalists to Toronto for a gala event at Roy Thomson Hall, where the national winner was to be announced.

I had never been involved in anything like it in my life. My challenge, along with school and the hospital, was to decide if I would travel to Toronto from Saskatchewan for that final award ceremony, with the bleeding a clear and present threat. I was still coughing up blood although it seemed to subside if I limited my movement and the speed at which I moved.

I had already decided nothing would be delayed or eliminated, and that included the flight to Toronto for the gala.

I prayed day and night that I would not have a bleeding episode during the event or traveling, which would have required hospitalization in another province.

I made the trek to Toronto, largely without a medical incident. Then, that night in Toronto, to my complete shock, I was announced the national winner … and I made it through with only mild bleeding.

It wasn't just winning the national prize that gave me much-needed momentum. It was winning after being told that it was far more important to set everything else aside and focus on my health.

That win let me know that all was not lost. If I focused on my response and I never stopped doing what I had my heart and mind set on, then anything was possible.

If I was to be taken out of the game of life it wouldn't occur with quiet consent.

In the picture of me with Frank you can see how gaunt and pale I was. But it gave me the much-needed secret ingredient: the momentum I needed to keep driving forward.

As a postscript to this story, Frank and I are, 25 years later, friends. My firm and I advise him. In fact, in 2021 he invited me to sit on the board of his new company, Stronach International Inc., focused on electric mobility (bikes, vehicles), agriculture and organic food.

The Saturday Sun, October 24, 1998

Magna-ficent win for future lawyer

Senate, tax reform plans worth scholarship

By PAUL CANTIN
Toronto Sun

Look out, Jean Chretien — the next prime minister of Canada could well be an articulate, exuberant law student from Saskatchewan preaching Senate and tax reform.

At a glitzy awards ceremony last night at Roy Thomson Hall, Christopher MacLeod, 28, was named winner of the Magna For Canada Scholarship for his winning essay on what he would do if he were prime minister.

MacLeod topped an impressive shortlist of 12 regional finalists for the prize package, which includes $10,000 to the winner, a matching grant to his school and a year's paid employment with Magna. The other finalists receive $5,000 and a summer job with Magna, and their essays have been published as a book, *As Prime Minister, I Would...*

"You provided us with a platform, but the real litmus test will be what we do with the scholarship," MacLeod told the scholarship's benefactor, Magna International chairman Frank Stronach, after the announcement. "We won't let you down."

Law studies

MacLeod, who is in his second year of law studies at the University of Saskatchewan, also holds a BA in political science and religious studies from the University of Regina, and studied for an MA in Islamic Studies in Morocco.

His essay, which was submitted along with more than 450 others for the fourth annual awards, lamented that people doubt our government has any "accountability, transparency or values." He proposed Senate reform, tax restructuring, an education program that spurred job creation and free dispersement of land to Canadian and foreign businesses who locate here.

'It was unbelievable'

The showbiz-style presentation featured performances from Winnipeg singer Chantal Kreviazuk, Celtic music innovators Leahy and classical violinist James Ehnes, as well as comedian Dave Broadfoot.

"It was unbelievable," said Richmond Hill resident and finalist Lara Richmond. Her essay lamented Canadians' lack of familiarity with their own country and advocated "awareness" as a way to foster "productive relationships."

"This is a wonderful way for students to express their views."

Along with MacLeod and Richmond, the other finalists were John Carpay of Calgary, Lorin Busaan of Blackfalds, Alta., Maryse Bouchard of Saint-Jean-sur-Richelieu, Luca Palladino of Lachine, Derek Zeisman of Kootenay, David Tarrant of St. John's, Charles Lafortune of Sudbury, Bradley MacKay of Huntsville, Bojan Pavlovic of Etobicoke and Eric Tam of Toronto.

"In this fast-changing world, we must stand on guard for thee. We must also invest in human capital, namely young Canadians," Stronach said.

— Greig Reekie, SUN

IMPRESSED WITH THE YOUNG GUY ... Magna International chairman Frank Stronach, right, last night greets Saskatchewan law student Christopher MacLeod, 28, who was named the winner of the Magna for Canada Scholarship.

The article from October 24, 1998 from the Toronto Sun.
Reprinted with the permission of the Toronto Sun/Postmedia Network.

I could have easily not attended class that first semester, or the event in Toronto. I could have put down the books and closed my eyes and rested. I did rest, eat, do physiotherapy, but I also never lost sight of the goals I had.

I lived by the principle and was prepared to die by it. I controlled my response, and my response was not to lose sight of what I set out to do.

That experience in 1997–1998 taught me a lot. Perhaps most important: life lessons are learned more from the challenges than the victories.

Whether you have a victory or a defeat the only thing to do is take stock and say "Next" and leave it to the history books.

> *To live a good life: We have the potential for it. If we learn to be indifferent to what makes no difference.*
> MARCUS AURELIUS

Don't overvalue your achievements or be diminished by your failures or failings. You have one life to live. Your job is to live it so fully that great stories are told about what you did with it.

Make your response to what happens to you bold and daring. It will forever change your world.

I'd also like to share stories of others with whom I have worked.

As mentioned elsewhere in this book, following my 2012 health crisis, I set up a not-for-profit organization: The Canadian Cystic Fibrosis Treatment Society (CCFTS) with the sole objective to secure and make available life-saving medications for any patient should their doctor prescribe it.

The CCFTS has pressed health charities, health insurance companies, big pharma, governments, and hospitals to ensure immediate access to and receipt of whatever medication or treatment a patient is prescribed.

There are 169 individuals in Canada with the same CF gene type as me. They all desperately needed Kalydeco. An analogy: if any of us were on a ship with

169 others, and the ship started to sink, any of us would stop at nothing to ensure those 169 got to shore, and survived!

My response to assist the other 169 individuals with that CF gene type was to secure access for them.

In advocating for public access to Kalydeco and the other gene modulators that eventually became available, additional voices were needed – specifically the voices of individuals who needed the other gene modulators.

Here are six examples of heroic women who epitomize the principle of this Lesson and advocated fearlessly and fiercely for themselves. These six chose to come forward in a public way very early on, with little to no support, joining in and leading press conferences and challenges to government when help was desperately needed for our cause of public access to these life-saving medications.

Each acted boldly and powerfully. Here are these champions.

Lilia

Born in Bulgaria, Lilia immigrated to Canada at age five. She had a diagnosis of CF, but faced even greater challenges at home where she faced abuse and neglect. By the age of 14 Lilia was taken by Child Protective Services. Lilia remained under the care of Child Protective Services until she was 19, the age at which all children who are under the care of the state "age out" and are sent out to fend for themselves.

Despite the challenges that are evident from the little I have told of her story, she ultimately responded with an incredible and heroic fight.

> *The happiness of your life depends on the quality of your thoughts.*
> MARCUS AURELIUS

By her early 30s Lilia was a student at university and her health was failing. Her health plan coverage while at school provided for a new medication called Orkambi until the plan was adjusted and Orkambi was no longer covered. Lilia was left without coverage.

Desperate to not fall through the cracks and lose the gene modulators life-line, she commenced a public fight with the government to secure access through the provincially-funded drug plan.

Melissa

An incredible woman and mother to two boys, Melissa had private insurance and was flourishing on Orkambi. She also lost her private coverage, fell off the medication and started to decline rapidly. Ultimately, with a lung function of less than 20% Melissa was on a lung transplant list.

Lilia and Melissa joined forces and commenced the first class-action lawsuit on behalf of CF patients in Canada. They led the charge. They became representative plaintiffs, challenging all levels of government and the relevant government agencies for violating the Canadian Charter of Rights and Freedoms, a fundamental element of the Canadian constitution.

> *You have power over your mind – not outside events. Realize this, and you will find strength.*
> MARCUS AURELIUS

While both did well on Orkambi they are now on the latest drug called Trikafta, which is a life-sustaining, game-changing medication. Both have seen significant improvements in their lung function.

When that lawsuit was launched in British Columbia, apart from the press, few showed up for the press conference other than my mother and a friend of Lilia's who also had CF.

The press was well aware of the government's position and came with hard-hitting questions, some bordering on nasty. Lilia and Melissa held up well and pursued relentlessly a public campaign for access.

They have been joined by others in various regions across Canada.

(Full disclosure: My firm Cambridge LLP commenced the class action with the firm George Douvelos DG Barristers in British Columbia.)

Madi

Madi was only 12 years old when she chose her own response to losing access to Kalydeco. She and her mother Beth launched a torrential downpour of advocacy efforts that set the standard for how patients advocate for themselves.

Madi ultimately pressed for and secured access to Kalydeco for provincial formularies. She is a testament to the power of one voice to move the dial and save countless lives.

Ella

Ella is a young girl from my home province of Saskatchewan who is wise and mature beyond her years. She has courageously stood up and spoken out, insisting that Orkambi and other medications that she and others need be made available for those that do not have a private benefits plan. She has yet to obtain access for herself but is tireless in her efforts.

Cassidy

Another young girl from Saskatchewan, and a true inspiration, Cassidy established Cassidy's Lemonade Stand and took it across the province, raising funds and awareness. Cassidy sat down with the premier of the province to push for access, and secured from him a commitment to do so in 100 days. We still have no access, but Cassidy and the others have not given up hope.

Victoria

Yet another courageous young soul that came forward was Victoria. She held press conferences and spoke out publicly in Ontario. Her voice was heard. In fact, she became the face of a provincial election campaign for patients who were denied access to life-sustaining medications. The social media campaign she was featured in helped raise awareness for and focused attention on the need to secure access to life sustaining medicine for CF patients.

Individual advocacy matters. Life is always about how you respond to the challenges you face. You are never alone. There are always many others facing the same situation as you. We all need examples, and these six provided early examples that helped shine a light on the path. As Ralph Waldo Emerson once said, "Do not go where the path may lead, go instead where there is no path and leave a trail."

The trail was blazed in part by these young women. Their leadership is really the foundation on which incredible advocacy efforts are rooted. They are examples of responding with wisdom, strength and courage.

I am thrilled to see that all around the world patients are raising their voices and advocating for themselves. In Canada the incredible advocacy group CF Get Loud was established with Steph Stavros, Jacob Jaramillo,

Mathew Van Camp and Beth Vanstone (Madi's mom) providing a platform and illustrating the power of collective advocacy.

All these individuals prove the point that you must be the CEO of your own health. And when you do, everyone rises with that tide.

LESSON NOTES

There is Power in Your Response

LESSON 4

Live in Day-Tight Compartments

Yes, you must acknowledge the past and the future. Don't forget the past and don't worry about the future ... but never dwell on either.

Your first job is to live in "day-tight compartments" – a term first coined by the great Canadian physician Sir William Osler to encourage people to concentrate on what lies directly at hand, rather than regret the past or be anxious about the future. It is one thing to say you control your response, but if you do not live in day-tight compartments, you will soon be overwhelmed.

> *Begin at once to live, and count each separate day as a separate life.*
>
> SENECA

That is why we have days. Anyone can deal with or survive anything for a day, but if you take the accumulated worries and fears from the past and the concerns of the unknown tomorrow, you will break (in any number of ways).

The beauty and the genius of life is that it begins

anew every 24 hours, and yes, every day is truly a new beginning.

"I have always been delighted at the prospect of a new day, a fresh try, one more start, with perhaps a bit of magic waiting somewhere behind the morning."
J. B. PRIESTLEY

True happiness is to enjoy the present, without anxious dependence upon the future, not to amuse ourselves with either hopes or fears but to rest satisfied with what we have, which is sufficient, for he that is so wants nothing.
SENECA

To be able to leave the failings of the past behind is not so hard. But to not be concerned about tomorrow, while still maintaining the dreams in your heart, now *that* is the work of champions.

In the context of a health crisis, it is so much more difficult. There are tests done daily over which you have no control. You can't prepare for blood-work. The result will determine if you are discharged from hospital or if you stay on for more tests, intrusions and procedures.

You see the pain in those you care for as they worry. You want to take away their worry, but the only thing that will take it away is your return to health and vitality.

Hospitals be damned! You must always be on guard

against getting dragged into a mindset of complacency. Living in day-tight compartments helps you combat that enemy.

It is in that hospital setting that you need, more than ever, not to worry about the future or fret over the past.

> *When you arise in the morning, think of what a precious privilege it is to be alive – to breathe, to think, to enjoy, to love.*
> MARCUS AURELIUS

Your bills and external pressures do not stop. Rent is still due on the first of the month. So is heat and power. If you've got a business, not only is payroll due every two weeks, but also individuals and families are counting on you to be sure they can take home the bacon. These are tough realities.

I would pray, meditate and concentrate on what was needed to be done to execute the plan for that day and that day alone.

The goal was simple: get my weight and my lung function up. Then get on the phone and help as many people solve their problems as I could.

To help banish distraction, fear and doubt, I focus on a mantra I read in a book called *Secret of the Ages*, published in 1925. It has many treasures that are worth reflecting on. One poem included in the book, "Thinking," is a great reminder for how to secure and ensure your days stand alone, and that fear and doubt are held at bay.

Thinking

If you think you are beaten, you are;
If you think you dare not, you don't;
If you'd like to win, but you think you can't,
It's almost a cinch you won't;
If you think you'll lose, you've lost,
For out in the world you'll find
Success begins with a fellow's will –
It's all in the state of mind.

Full many a race is lost
Ere even a race is run,
And many a coward fails
Ere even his work's begun.
Think big, and your deeds will grow,
Think small and you fall behind,
Think that you can, and you will;
It's all in the state of mind.

If you think you are outclassed, you are;
You've got to think high to rise;
You've got to be sure of yourself before
You can ever win a prize.
Life's battle doesn't always go
To the stronger or faster man;
But sooner or later, the man who wins
Is the fellow who thinks he can.

—Walter D. Wintle

LESSON NOTES

Live in Day-Tight Compartments

LESSON 5

Dream Big and Write It Down

Start by *dreaming big*: Whatever you can conceive or imagine and you believe … you can achieve.

This cannot be overestimated or over-stated enough. If you're sick and just can't get out of your own hospital bed, then you need to focus on dreaming.

Television, movies, books – they contain the dreams and imaginations of others.

In *your* mind paint a Picasso, a Rembrandt. The future is truly a blank slate. Get to work and dream. Dream as though there is no illness or healthcare crisis in front of you. Create imaginary castles in the sky where you are the king or queen or head of state.

As the Queen says to Alice in *Through the Looking Glass*: "I've believed as many as six impossible things before breakfast." She is right. Everything great that was ever done started in someone's imagination: planes, trains, automobiles, the Sistine chapel, running the 4-minute mile …

This is your time, your chance to answer this question: "What would I do if I knew I could not fail?"

Assuming that there was no illness to impede you, no financial burden or barrier, no limits in time or space – what then, would you do? You need to inspire yourself. Let your imagination drive you.

For me, I wanted to get back to work to practice law, advocating for clients whether in the boardroom or the courtroom.

To get there, I needed to breathe without the aid of supplementary oxygen. My lung function was less than 30% FEV1. The reality was it had been at sub-50% for a long time.

My weight at my healthiest had never been above 160 pounds in all my 42 years.

My dream, the goal I set for myself (which was considered to be well beyond reach by any medical professional) was a weight of 165 pounds and a lung function of 65% as measured by FEV1. (This was prior to the advent of gene modulating precision medicine. The world is now a very different place.)

But in the summer of 2012, falling below 30% when you are over 40 years of age was "Grim Reaper" time.

Thus the reason for dreaming big dreams. Mine was not realistic, and it was not meant to be. It was a dream that seemed almost impossible at the time, which is why I took it on.

It's vital to take your dreams and ideas out of your head and place them in the real world, where they can flourish and grow. In my hospital room there was a small whiteboard. There's one in every room. On it, they put the name of the nurse or doctor for each shift.

I took that white board and wrote down my goals: the simplest goals I could have. Not because I didn't have large, meaningful, meaty goals, but in that moment, all I wanted to do was hit these two milestones on which all else rested.

165 pounds

65% FEV1

Never, Ever Give Up … EVER.

Both goals were unrealistic when I posted them – and for everyone at the hospital to see. I had never been 165 pounds, ever. I was also sicker at this point than I had ever been.

My average weight was 155–160 pounds When I fell below 155 I got sick like clockwork. This time I was below 150. I was eating six thousand calories a day and barely keeping my weight at 147.

I knew I had to take a drastic step. I set the goal at 165 pounds because I've always wanted to get there, but had never been there. As for the pulmonary score of 65 FEV1, the last time I saw it was in 2000.

I was currently on 4 litres of supplementary oxygen

a minute and my FEV1 score on admission was less than 30%. Little did I know that my lung function had been in the 30s for a significant period of time.

> *First say to yourself what you would be; and then do what you have to do.*
> EPICTETUS

Ultimately, the first goal was achieved. The second: that of hitting 65% FEV1, remains my challenge.

In my race to 65% I have been as high as 60%, but the 65 that I placed on that whiteboard, well, it is still not yet within my grasp! But the operative word is *yet*!

Rick Hansen, the famous Canadian who went around the world in a wheelchair in the 1980s to raise money and awareness for spinal injuries, did an amazing interview with journalist Pamela Wallin that I will never forget. In essence, he said that he truly believed he will walk again.

Her question was a legitimate one, here paraphrased: You believe you will walk again, but isn't that just a positive attitude? Surely you don't believe that you'll actually walk again?

His response struck me and has stuck with me. He reiterated that he believes that he will walk again, and that through research spinal cord injuries can be overcome.

The look on his face and in his eyes said everything we needed to know. He was convinced of it. To this day, he has not yet walked, but I believe he ultimately will. I am certain that he believes he will walk again and that others with spinal cord injuries will as well.

I also truly believe that I will get to 65% FEV1 with credit to my medical team at St. Mike's.

Dr. Tullis, in as convincing a voice as I told her I would do it, said to me in a matter-of-fact tone that she would not rule out anything in my case. Her manner of speaking was sincere – with the clear belief that anything is truly possible.

I mean literally *anything* is possible.

To quote Yoda, when he was training Luke Skywalker in the *Empire Strikes Back*: "Do or do not; there is no try."

To this day I write down my goals. Not simply goals for my health, I write down goals every week in the following five areas:

- Health
- Finance/Business
- Spirituality
- Community
- Family

These goals need to be detailed and in-depth. They need to be on the far outskirts of what is realistic. Do not think small. Think 10X. Set goals so large and vast that they live firmly in your imagination. Envision them. Then bring them to life.

If someone says you cannot do it, then *that* is what you should try to do. And always remember the achievements of others who accomplished that which was once considered impossible.

> *Impossible is a word to be found only in the dictionary of fools.*
> NAPOLEON BONAPARTE

Beginning in 1886 a serious sports goal was imagined: running the mile in under 4 minutes. No one had ever done it, no one had even come close, and it would be another 60 years before anyone achieved it.

It was thought that it would take ideal conditions of 68 degrees Fahrenheit, perfect weather, and no wind. The runner would need to have talent and skill, with vast experience and training (and a team of coaches).

Then on 6 May 1954, on a cold, wet day in Oxford, England, Roger Bannister broke the 4-minute mile in 3 minutes and 59.4 seconds.

Bannister was considered a lone wolf who trained with unorthodox methods. Yet, he was the one who broke through the barrier … and fundamentally changed the perception of what was possible.

Within 46 days of Bannister's record, John Landy in Australia had broken the 4-minute mile as well. Today over 1,000 people have run a mile in under 4 minutes.

How did Bannister break through that "impenetrable" ceiling? It is this unique force that anyone who has a health condition needs to capture.

The reality is that life with a serious, chronic, or

terminal health condition is akin to the 4-minute mile, prior to 1954.

It simply had never been done. Much like when Ron, who I referred to earlier, ran the Penticton Ironman in under 10 hours. He had CF and it simply should not have been possible. Now others have done it, including Ontario's Lisa Bentley, who has won 11 Ironman competitions.

Be discriminating about what images and ideas you permit into your mind.
EPICTETUS

CF was a condition that was once a terminal childhood illness. Youngsters were not focused on post-secondary education, because it was believed that they would pass on early, so why put in the effort? Thankfully, this belief has changed for many.

Roger Bannister is a northern star, and his lesson should not be forgotten. Set your goals in the healthcare context like the 4-minute mile – before Bannister shattered it.

For me, it was 65% FEV1 lung function. Although I do not have that number now… I know, as sure as the night follows day … I will get it back … just like Rick Hansen is convinced he will walk again. Every health challenge that appears insurmountable is possible to achieve. It is always possible.

That is why it is so critical to write down one's goals, particularly the impossible ones. Those goals that seem to be impossible – when firmly rooted in your heart and mind and soul, such that you are prepared to stake your life on it, then just when you are at the end of your tether – it's then that the goals can be achieved.

If a man knows not to which port he sails, no wind is favourable.
SENECA

To date, I do not believe Rick has hit his goal, but I promise you … he will.

I haven't returned to 65% FEV1 … but I promise you … I will.

> "Imagination is more important than knowledge. For knowledge is limited, whereas imagination embraces the entire world, stimulating progress, giving birth to evolution."

Einstein was right.

LESSON NOTES

Dream Big and Write It Down

LESSON 6

Get Up, Dress Up and Show Up

I think the words in this lesson title are from Paulo Coelho, author of *The Alchemist.*

90% of life's moments happen when you least expect them. In the context of a hospital stay or a health crisis, this has more meaning and import than you can imagine.

First: Get up.

This simple act may well be the one thing you can actually immediately realize in a hospital, unless, of course, you are on life support or immobilized.

When you ache all over and you simply can't move … if you're so sick they insist you stay in bed, then you know that what you need to do is rest and recover. But that doesn't mean you can't get up at the beginning of the day. That will send a message to yourself and all those around you.

Unless you are in a coma, get up, shower, or wash yourself in a sink. Crawl if you have to, but *get up*. Shower, shave, groom. You can go back to bed – in fact, you probably should, because your body needs rest.

In my case, I would then make the bed … not like the orderlies do with the sheets as tight as a trampoline. I would pull up the sheets and put the bedspread up so it wasn't messy. This is an ill layman's attempt to prove a point more to myself than to the outside world.

Your mind will take the shape of what you frequently hold in thought, for the human spirit is coloured by such impressions.
MARCUS AURELIUS

I would get up every morning regardless of how bad I felt and wash, dress, and if possible take off the oxygen and make my way to the coffee shop across the street. Exhausted when I arrived there, I felt like shit, or death warmed over! (The best non-medical way to describe it.)

It was hard. I wanted nothing more than to be in bed. I was exhausted before I got up. The coffee helped. Sitting down to drink it, to catch my breath and focus on that day and that day alone, also helped.

The power of rising up can never be overstated. It lets you take control of your day. A day is a lifetime. So much can happen. You need to be up and ready to seize the moment, any moment, that passes by and that gives you a lift.

At St. Mike's Hospital, I would get up before the 7 a.m. shift change. I wanted to be sure those coming onto shift knew I was in the fight. I wanted those leaving the shift to go home knowing there was fight still left in this guy.

I wanted *me* to know that whatever I could do, I was doing. I needed to prove to myself that there was still fight left in me.

On my return to the hospital ward after that coffee, I would occasionally buy donuts for the staff. You need to reverse-engineer the care program. If you are leading the team, you need to care for the caregiver.

Recall, I am under 150 pounds I can't breathe well without 4 litres of oxygen a minute. My oxygen would fall below 90, which I'm told is not good. The average person is 99–100, even after or during exercise.

I would return to the room exhausted, but this time I would be dressed and lie on top of the bed sheets. I would pick up the phone. Let people, but most importantly, myself know that I was still in the game.

You must send a message that you are in command of your day. I did this every day, without fail. Not because I felt well or could even dress in a proper manner.

One particularly rough day, I was wearing a suit and tie, and was on the edge of my bed. I had been at the hospital for several weeks and nothing was improving. I was barely at 149 pounds and that was eating thousands of calories a day.

It was just after morning shift change. I knew virtually all the staff: orderlies, interns, nurses, porters, everyone. I liked everyone without exception. They cared for each patient as though we were members of their family.

> *It is not death a man should fear, but he should fear never beginning to live.*
> MARCUS AURELIUS

That particular day, a nurse I liked, she who was chatty and liked to talk, came into my room. She meant well, but I think she was beginning to think that my approach may have been denial and that I needed to come to grips with my own mortality.

She told me the story of another patient much like me, she said. That patient did well, but, after 30 days, became sick and then he died. His death was quick and it was sudden. She said I may need to come to grips with the fact that I won't be getting better and that this disease has killed many who were healthier than me. She meant it in the best way possible.

I remember the conversation well. It was one of those moments where the truth, as the world knows it and what you want the truth to be, is put to you as a choice.

You get to decide. Is she right? Am I just wasting my energy on a frolic? Is this sheer silliness to those around me? Have I become a caricature of myself and am I actually doing no favours by not accepting the reality of this condition and finding a way to move on in the next stage of my life?

Those thoughts found no fertile ground in my thinking process. Let's call her Jane. I said to her: "Jane, I respect you and your views, but here is the rule in this room. Option A, that goal (I pointed to the white board on the wall) will be met. Option B is to get carried out in a body bag.

"You can ask me to leave the hospital but we have one route. Meet that goal or die trying. If you are right and death is a real possibility, then it's time to double-down on the unrealistic and make it real."

Ironically, she gave me added enthusiasm for my project, which I affectionately referred to as the Campaign for Health.

Another tactic I utilized is never telling anyone I was sick or in the hospital. Some people found out. Some, like my law partners, I had to tell.

I was dealing with client calls all day, every day, as well as firm business. Having my phone on, constantly on the phone helping clients manage the crises that they faced, kept me in the game. It was as critical to my mind-set as the volumes of intravenous meds were to the physical fight against the infection.

I had two external lifelines:

One: The internal management of my firm. No one mentioned the hospital. We only focused on work: account receivables, files, management, and great results for clients.

Two: Dealing directly with clients on their matters.

Fortunately, for me, I can work lying on my back or sitting upright in bed for the vast majority of my activities. I do not underestimate nor will I fail to acknowledge the vast blessings that have been given to me.

One dear friend and client, Ross, had a project he was working on that had some challenges at the pre-construction stage. He and I would speak every morning at 7:30 to walk through what he needed to do and how we could get to the end-zone. He had no idea how much that helped *me* get to the end-zone.

It is so critical to get out of your head and out of your own way.

A great Chinese parable rings so true about how to re-focus away from your own problems by assisting others to solve theirs.

It involves a woman whose only son died. In her grief she went to a holy man and asked, "What prayers, what magical incantations do you have to bring my son back to life?"

Instead of sending her away or dismissing her, he said: "Fetch me a mustard seed from a home that has never known sorrow, to drive the sorrow out of your own life." The woman went off at once in search of that magical mustard seed.

She came first to a splendid mansion, knocked at the door, and said, "I am looking for a home that has never known sorrow. Is this such a place? It is very important to me."

They told her, "You've certainly come to the wrong place." They began to describe all the tragedy that had recently befallen them.

The woman said to herself, "Who better to help these poor unfortunate people than I, who have had misfortune of my own?"

He who has resolved to conquer or die is seldom conquered.
PIERRE CORNEILLE

She stayed to comfort them, and then went on in search of a home that had never known sorrow. But wherever she turned, in hotels, mansions, hovels and in other places, she found one tale after another of sadness and misfortune.

The woman became so involved in helping others cope with their sorrows that she eventually let go of her own. She would later come to understand that it was the quest to find the magical mustard seed that drove away her suffering.

Everyone suffers in a multitude of ways. Every story of human suffering is different and real.

Look outside your tent to heal yourself. Look for the mustard seed and do not wallow in your own sorrow.

As American author, spiritual writer, and Franciscan Father Richard Rohr has said, life and faith involve great suffering and great love. That is the essence of the Paschal mystery in the Christian faith.

A life well-lived will have healthy doses of both.

Remember: Get Up, Dress Up, Show Up. Eventually, momentum arrives and when she does, you need to be ready to seize the day.

LESSON NOTES

Get Up, Dress Up and Show Up

LESSON 7

The Power of Prayer

As is evident, I am a firm believer in the power of prayer. I believe that everyone on this planet, and every creature great and small, has been created with divine intent. Whatever you face in life, your faith system will sustain you – whatever your faith system may be.

I hope that everyone has had the privilege of knowing, as the psalmist says in Psalm 139, the feeling of being "fearfully and wonderfully made."

In my case, I'm a Christian of the Catholic faith. Albeit an imperfect one, but it's an ideal I aspire to live up to and a north star by which I try to set my actions. It is a belief system I've chosen to subscribe to and strive to meet.

To those who criticize me, as the Stoics have said: "You are correct in my fault, the only issue I take is that you have missed so many more faults."

Prayer is what you feel compelled to do in your darkest moments. It also arises in those awe-inspiring moments when you are overwhelmed by the sheer beauty of life and nature. It is born when you witness a feat of extreme human endurance and the only recourse is to look up towards the heavens, or fall to your knees and give thanks for the events in your life or that you have been afforded an opportunity to witness.

Prayer is grounded in gratitude for the blessings we have received and is also a very simple request for the strength we may need to overcome our darkest moments.

Here are examples for me of the power of prayer.

Gethsemane Prayer

What I call the Gethsemane Prayer arises when you are at the end of your tether and have absolutely no place else to go. This is a personal prayer made by you to a Greater Power.

It is a prayer made by people of faith and also by those who have never had a discernible connection to a religious faith.

It is an emotional prayer grounded in fear and desperation. It is the prayer made by the religious and those who are not, by those who have no belief and those who do. It's a prayer for when one is at the end of the line.

It is also the prayer that a very human Jesus made the evening before he was crucified. He walked away from the disciples. On his own, he fell to his knees and wept. He prayed that the problems of his life and the world would pass him by with the ultimate refrain: "Father, let this cup pass me by … not my will, but yours be done."

It is a powerful moment in the Christian tradition because it is a clear expression of the humanity of Jesus. Weak and afraid, he was crying to his heavenly father that he not have to endure any suffering … that this can all end.

It is not an intellectual, theological prayer. Raw and filled with human emotion, it is the prayer of a man experiencing real fear, thus the tears and cry and plea that this "cup" pass him by.

It is not a quick prayer but a heart-wrenching scene followed by betrayal of his closest disciples, and ultimately his death.

This is the power of prayer when you are simply sick and tired of being sick and tired.

The fact is you can carry anything for a day… That's why we live in day-tight compartments, as I wrote about earlier. The lesson of living in day-tight compartments takes incredible discipline and consistency which almost no one can do – and certainly not me!

It's when the future and the worries about what might happen collide with what has happened in the past. It weighs on your shoulders as you face the formidable and daunting moment in which you stand – the present.

It is now, at this moment, when you've got nothing left and you feel like you can't go on. It is then that you are drawn to your knees and pray to your Maker for strength.

What ought one to say then as each hardship comes? I was practicing for this, I was training for this.
EPICTETUS

I remember as clear as night follows day, when I had a powerful religious experience that left an indelible imprint on my soul and my heart, seared in my memory for all time. It occurred in the fall of 1997 during the hospital stay I spoke about in Lesson 3.

It was when I was 28 years old, having just been accepted into law school. I could not have been more excited for what the future held. I had moved back to my home town of Saskatoon, Saskatchewan. The world and the future were absolutely and positively brilliant.

I described the bleeding earlier. In my gut I knew it was bad. If you're drowning, you can get out of the water, or at least know that when you get to dry land you'll be safe. I had no such assurances about my bleeding.

I was admitted and discharged and re-admitted, but by late October, well through the first semester, the bleeding simply would not stop.

I had been coughing blood incessantly for weeks. Finally, the resident said to me that we needed to do a bronchoscopy to determine where the bleed is and what we might do to stop it.

She had the look that comes when someone has tried everything possible and nothing seems to work. There was nothing more that she could do.

If anyone tells you that a certain person speaks ill of you, do not make excuses about what is said but answer, 'He was ignorant of my other faults, else he would not have mentioned these alone.'

EPICTETUS

I was about to go in for a bronchoscopy. I would not wish the procedure on anyone. I certainly hope the procedure has improved over the past 25 years.

In order for you to breathe consciously, the team is not able to put you under because they're sticking a scope down your throat into your lungs to determine where the bleeding is. Of course, because your body and lungs vigorously react, there's one person at your feet and another at your head to turn you over every few seconds when the gagging is extreme and you need to vomit or cough. They flip you over so you don't choke on your own bile or whatever it is you're coughing up and out.

My mom was in the room with the resident who was in charge of the bronchoscopy.

Prior to going into the room for the procedure, on the cusp of first semester final exams worth 100% of the grade, I simply wasn't sure if I had any steam left.

I also hate hospitals and I dread medical procedures. I'm not proud of it but I have an inordinate fear of needles.

Heading in to the procedure, I went on my knees and I prayed: "God, I'm out of steam. I'm in your hands. If this is all you've got written for me, then take your servant. I ask that you give me the strength and courage to get through this day, but if it's not in the cards or your will, then give me peace."

It was in that moment that I experienced something I've never felt before and never since.

An overwhelming sense of security covered my entire body. Every ounce of fear and trembling vanished. I was left with an incredible sense of empowerment and strength that absolutely did not come from within.

To say that I had no fear would be to understate it. It was far more than simply no fear of this procedure. In fact, I gave the resident a pep talk and told her it would be fine and she would do a great job and I believed it! Frankly, it was true. She did.

I remember the flips back-and-forth from my back to my stomach throughout and seeing her face and my mother's and again the look on their faces of helplessness that one feels when there was so little they can do.

But in that moment that incredible sense of security and strength that had come upon me did not leave until I was returning to the room and then everything went back to normal.

I have had other equally traumatic experiences where I prayed but *sensed* that nothing occurred, and *just had to trust that God was still working despite my inability to immediately perceive it.*

I would be a liar if I did not tell that story as the absolute proof, for me, of the power of prayer in my life at that moment in time.

To this day, I am drawn back to that moment and am always wondering what happened, and how do I get back that sense that I can only describe as truly being without fear.

The phrase used 365 times in both *The Old* and *The New Testament* is "Be not afraid." I learned this from one of my dear friends, Peter, on his Facebook post, so I'll accept it as a fact! Interesting that 365 parallels the exact number of days in a year. Thus, Lesson 4, live in day-tight compartments … without fear. Perhaps the absence of fear is not simply no fear, but peace.

The last parting statement Jesus gives to his disciples and the early church on the Pentecost was, "Peace I leave with you; my peace I give you."

That is the peace that comes from a deep trust in God and in that moment we find an absence of fear. It is peace that fills the void.

This is not unique to Christianity. The standard greeting of one Muslim believer to another is: *A' Salaamu Aleikum*. Or, may the peace be to you that comes from surrendering your will to the will of God.

Or in the Jewish faith: *Shalom* or Peace.

The Power of Others Praying for You

My second example is not of me praying, but of others praying for me and the power that has.

Let's be clear, praying for others is essential not simply because it lets us do something when there appears to be almost nothing that we can do, but because the one you pray for knows it. They feel it and with such collective prayer mountains can be moved.

As I have described during the story of my extensive 2012 hospitalization, my lung function had fallen below 30% making me eligible for a lung transplant. I knew that people in churches, mosques and synagogues and those who had no formal place to worship all were praying for me. I could feel it in my bones. I knew it because people called me and told me they were praying for me. I knew it because I had attended hundreds of vesper prayers at the altar and prayed with others as names were called out and notes left in the basket at Mass were read out loud.

On Sunday, 21 September 2012 my mother, Joan Lidington, called me from Saskatchewan. My mother is an incredible woman of faith. My faith has been cultivated in large part by her humble and clear example of a life of faith. Her servant leadership is a topic for another day.

That Sunday morning, she and I had happened to

be watching the same video of a great sermon titled "Pray Boldly."

As Goethe said: "Boldness has genius, magic, and power in it." Well, it certainly did on that September day.

And even in our sleep, pain which cannot forget, falls drop by drop upon the heart, until, in our own despair, against our will, comes wisdom through the awful grace of God.
AESCHYLUS

Both my mom and I had been moved by the sermon that day.

She said: "Chris, I've been praying boldly and I know, I just know, something amazing is going to happen this week. Everyone at church has been praying for you and also those of little faith have been praying for you." People would come up to her and say: "We're praying for Chris."

I can honestly say it's phenomenally empowering to know that people are praying for you.

We ended the conversation with her saying, "Everything will be fine. Something is going to happen this week to turn this around. *I just know it.*" It was said with that degree of certainty that comes from knowing something is true at its core.

I replied that I hoped she was right! Little did I know how right she was.

The next morning at 9 a.m. Dr. Tullis came into the room and told me the news I've outlined earlier in these pages.

Well I know that most, if not everyone, will say that this is not a miracle or the work of God, but of hard science that started in 1989, and that the drug was on the market ready before anyone prayed for me.

All I know is that on the timeline of my life, I can attest to this: prayers were made and prayers were answered.

I had no idea I had that particular type of gene; I had never heard of it or the research leading to a CFTR gene modulator that could in fact normalize my genetic defect.

Life is about choices and I choose to believe that it was the power of prayers answered that helped to facilitate that event in my life.

At the end of the day we are all instruments of a greater power, if we choose to believe that to be the case.

As the Greek tragedian Aeschylus said about pain and suffering, it is not simply the larger moments that cover the horizon of one's life but the small insidious events that tire us out.

The wisdom I take from my story and the moments of prayer made by myself and others is that the awful grace of God can be found in prayer.

As country star Garth Brooks more recently added: "Sometimes I thank God for unanswered prayers; Remember when you're talking to the man upstairs; That just because He doesn't answer doesn't mean He don't care; Some of God's greatest gifts are unanswered prayers."

LESSON NOTES

The Power of Prayer

LESSON 8

The Power of Smiling and Laughing

Nowhere does the smile, and its power, have greater clarity or currency than in the hospital, where all around you people are dying or worrying that they might be.

Time spent as an in-patient generates endless material for *Seinfeld*. The ordinary is bizarre. Laughing and finding humour in the insane and the crazy is mandatory for survival. The best material, of course, comes when you are blessed with the opportunity to share a room with another patient.

I was once hospitalized with a significant blockage in my abdomen and gut. To move it I had to drink multiple two-litre containers of Pro Max over several days. (Anyone who has had a colonoscopy will know what this is. It is the drink you consume prior to the procedure to clean out your gut.)

It needs to be drunk cold and it leaves you shivering and freezing … and continuously "cleansing" (that's the nicest way I can put that) your gut by going to the washroom. When that isn't enough (and in my case it was not) the hospital staff gives you an enema, so that you are eliminating the obstruction in your gut from both ends.

We all sorely complain of the shortness of time, and yet have much more than we know what to do with. Our lives are either spent in doing nothing at all, or in doing nothing to the purpose, or in doing nothing that we ought to do. We are always complaining that our days are few, and acting as though there would be no end to them.

SENECA

After one nurse had given me no less than four or five enemas, she came into the room while my gown was open. She apologized.

I started to laugh: "After everything we've been through together I should probably have your phone number."

At one point a seriously disabled young man who was a patient at the children's hospital down the street turned 18. The rule is you get transferred out of Sick Kids as soon as you turn 18. Ward 6B is not pleasant if you're an adult, let alone a severely disabled kid coming from the children's hospital which is child-friendly. His family insisted on spending the night with him (or us). The couple argued with each other over which family member should spend the night in the room. Their argument ensued at a high pitch while I was on the phone pressing the government for access to the medication Kalydeco, which I wrote about earlier. I was also speaking at a high pitch. The hospital room, with me on a phone and the family also in the room arguing with each other, was a scene to behold!

I was using the bathroom in the room as my "office" to secure some form of privacy for discussing sensitive topics.

I came out of my office arguing with someone on the phone, wearing my boxers and a T-shirt that said "Superman." I had socks but no shoes on, with my IV pole in tow, trying to untangle the tubing that was wrapped around the wheel.

The nurse came in and said: "This is a hospital, and it's a gong show in here. You people need to quiet down!" She laughed and closed the door.

I looked around and started laughing. The family did too. It *was* a gong show in our room. But as they say … the show must go on.

What gives the hospital in-patient stay such rich material for humour is the vulnerability of the patients. You are fully exposed, walking around with tubes in your arms, or being prodded up, down, and under.

Following the enemas I was put on a gurney and taken down for a colonoscopy.

The guy next to me and I were discussing what was in store for us, as neither of us had been through a colonoscopy before.

He said to me: "Do you realize we are having a legitimate discussion about that guy over there sticking a camera up our ass? And we are willingly undressing for it?"

He had me howling.

Cry, whine, complain, or laugh. You will likely do all. When you're too sick to laugh, because it hurts when you do, then smile … even if it's a faint smile. It will lift up your spirits, and those of the people around you.

Everyone can laugh and smile when they feel good. That's easy. But God and the angels will part the sea for the one who is out of steam and losing the breath of life and still laughs and smiles, simply glad that they remain in the ring.

That is what moves mountains and shapes the human soul.

All life is finite. But it is the immediacy of the end that grips your attention. This knowledge gives character to those shaped by slow pain or the realization that life is limited.

Smile

Smile, though your heart is aching
Smile, even though it's breaking
When there are clouds in the sky
You'll get by

— John Turner and Geoffrey Parson

LESSON NOTES

The Power of Smiling and Laughing

LESSON 9

Never Give Up!

Never give up. Ever. It is simple. It is non-optional.

It is inevitable that at some point you will pass on to the next world. The good news about your passing and mine is that we will meet and be with our Maker.

The entire genius and the mystery and the success of life is in the struggle. It's climbing up that hill with a 50-pound pack on your back, with not enough oxygen or strength to get there.

It's the struggles and the race to the finish line with all its hurdles. It's when you know you're down, and so does the entire world … and they are sure you will never get up … and you keep on keeping on.

There are so many instances of individuals who in small ways simply tried to overcome, and in so doing, they did overcome. They proved what they are made of. They exhibited grit, resilience and drive unknown in the common hours.

Whether they made it or not, it is the resilience and the determination that casts a light for the world to see.

In every instance, when I have thought the chips were down (and they were), and all hope seemed to be lost (and from my vantage point it clearly was), that is when the victory comes. And if it doesn't, well that's what the living is for.

When Napoleon set out to conquer Europe east of the French Alps, many in the French army advised that trekking an army through the French alps could never be done. He replied: "There shall be no Alps."

When knocked down five times, you must get up six times.

David Goggins is a writer and individual for whom I have great respect. He tells his story in *Can't Hurt Me: Master Your Mind and Defy the Odds*. Beaten, abused, with no self-confidence, filled with self-doubt, he ultimately joined the US Navy and became a Seal. He failed Seal training twice before passing on his third try.

His point is that when you are completely out of fuel, it is then that you realize you've still got 40% more left in the tank:

> "Once you know that to be true, it's simply a matter of stretching your pain tolerance, letting go of your identity and all your self-limiting stories, so you can get to 60 percent, then 80 percent and beyond without giving up. I call this The 40% Rule, and the reason it's so

> powerful is that if you follow it, you will unlock your mind to new levels of performance and excellence in sports and in life, and your rewards will run far deeper than mere material success. The 40% Rule can be applied to everything we do. Because in life almost nothing will turn out exactly as we hope. There are always challenges, and whether we are at work or school, or feeling tested within our most intimate or important relationships, we will all be tempted to walk away from commitments, give up on our goals and dreams, and sell our own happiness short at some point. Because we will feel empty, like we have no more to give, when we haven't tapped even half of the treasure buried deep in our minds, hearts, and souls."

The battle I wage, and that all CF patients wage, is the simplest of struggles.

There is no magic or mystery or great event that hasn't been done before. It is simply a struggle to get sufficient oxygen in your lungs to get up the hill, to climb to the mountaintop and to see the other side.

Eric Thomas, a trainer of elite athletes and corporate executives, sums up what you need to succeed. "When you want to succeed as bad as you want to breathe, then you will be successful," he says.

He tells the story of an old wise man sitting by the

sea. He is watching a young athlete train at mid-day running up and down the beach. He calls him over and says, if you want to learn and to know the secret to success meet me here, tomorrow, at 5 a.m.

At 4:59 a.m. the young man shows up. The wise man tells him to follow him into the ocean. When they are up to their chest in water, the old man takes his student's head and pushes it under water and holds it there for close to a minute. Struggling to breathe, the young man finally exerts enough strength and force to push the old man away and screams at him…. "What are you doing?… you're trying to kill me!"

The old man replies, "I've taught you a lesson that you won't soon forget. When you want it … anything in life … as bad as you want to breathe, that is what you need to succeed."

Lives have been lost because CF got in the way of that very human drive to simply breathe. You can imagine the real struggle waged by these warriors for life.

Even if it's simply to breathe with ease, as you fight the infection that results from years of internal battles.

Can damaged lung tissue become healthy again? My simpleton approach is that the body rejuvenates itself every seven years. Cells die and are born again. The body is constantly healing and repairing and regenerating. Somewhere in that process is room for healing and for rebirth.

Never give up. Ever. Let someone else count you out and declare you dead. But that should never be you.

> *The world turns aside to let any man pass who knows where he is going.*
> EPICTETUS

Recall Courtney, from earlier in these pages. That kid had attitude and uncommon resilience. The light that he left in the world still shines bright and clear. There are hundreds of others that I have known and that we have lost. Their light and their memories fill the heavens. They leave their inspiration behind, for us.

Another is a gentleman I'll call Garth. He was older than me and had what I think was cerebral palsy. He was exceptionally bright, overweight, and would sweat profusely. He always wore a suit and his tie was tied loosely on his chest. He presented himself as if he was in the battle of the century.

He died too young, but my memory of Garth is of a guy who had a lot of hard cards dealt to him. He never complained or left any indication that he felt sorry for himself, or that anyone else should either. He laughed a hearty laugh and smiled a warm smile.

Garth and I had dozens of long dinners in the campus dining room. He was dedicated to his studies and was writing his thesis on a liberation theology for the disabled, a school of Christian theology that explores liberating people who are oppressed or downtrodden. It originates in Latin America in the Catholic Church. Its focus is on the marginalized, the dispossessed, and those souls left behind and forgotten.

You may fetter my leg, but Zeus himself cannot get the better of my free will.
EPICTETUS

He was focusing on what he could do for others, as in Lesson 3. That was the power in his response to his condition.

The challenge with a condition like CF, or any chronic terminal condition, is that people simply become sick and tired of being sick and tired. It never ends. Ultimately, you feel that you just can't keep the fight going.

I can understand how you can run out of steam. But I also know that you simply can never give up. Ever!

I have been blessed. To date I have not run out of steam. At the 11th hour, and clearly my darkest hour, I was given access to a game-changing wonder drug that keeps me in the fight. We now have a drug that makes CF a chronic condition, not a terminal condition.

But make no mistake: The fight goes on. It will continue until we have a cure.

Until we get there – and we will – we must fight with every ounce of energy we have, and when we do run out of energy, then we must pray for strength unknown in ordinary times.

That's why sports is such a great analogy for never giving up. Think of the games where one side was down. They were counted out and no one thought they would make it. As the basketball player Michael Jordan once said: "I never lost a game, I just ran out of time."

That is never giving up. Let the clock count you out – not your will.

I keep two posters on my wall at work. One has written in white letters on a dark backdrop:

"You will not get much done if you only grind on days you feel good."

The other is the famous quote from Teddy Roosevelt referred to as the "Man in the Arena":

> *A gem cannot be polished without friction, nor a man perfected without trials.*
> SENECA

> "It is not the critic who counts; not the man who points out how the strong man stumbles, or where the doer of deeds could have done them better. The credit belongs to the man who is actually in the arena, whose face is marred by dust and sweat and blood; who strives valiantly; who errs, who comes short again and again, because there is no effort without error and shortcoming; but who does actually strive to do the deeds; who knows great enthusiasms, the great devotions; who spends himself in a worthy cause; who at the best knows in the end the triumph of high achievement, and who at

the worst, if he fails, at least fails while daring greatly, so that his place shall never be with those cold and timid souls who neither know victory nor defeat."

LESSON NOTES

Never Give Up!

LESSON 10

Never Better

When asked how you are today … pause, and respond, "Never Better." It does wonders for your soul and touches the recipient whether they know it or not.

It's a frame of mind, an approach to life, and a tight, sharp, crisp way of expressing it to anyone around you. To have the "Never Better" approach to life is to live each moment as though it were the only one you had. At this moment you really are "Never Better" than you've ever been before.

> *It is not because things are difficult that we do not dare, it is because we do not dare that things are difficult.*
> SENECA

While I had this way of thinking, I did not have the term to express it … until I met my dear friend and mentor, Dennis Mills.

Dennis is a force of nature. As a former senior veteran of Parliament Hill in Ottawa once said: "Getting in the way of Dennis Mills when he has set his sight on a destination is simply not worth the energy, nor does anyone have that much energy.

The only recourse is to get out of the way or get on the train and go for the ride."

I first met Dennis in the summer of 1989 when I went with 27 others from Western Canada to work on Parliament Hill for a summer.

The trials you encounter will introduce you to your strengths. Remain steadfast...and one day you will build something that endures: something worthy of your potential.
EPICTETUS

Dennis and I became dear friends over the following 30 years. He taught me much, but the simple articulation of a life-saving and life-giving philosophy may be one of his greatest gifts to me. Those two simple words give voice to a philosophy of life. After years of carrying this mantra, I can personally attest to its life-affirming power.

If you are in the fight of your life and death is too close for comfort ... you need to offer these two words as your response, always – not just sometimes or when the mood takes you. Always.

To understand this genesis we need to go back to the 1960s when Dennis met Stuart Lawson, who worked at St. Michael's College School in Toronto. In the words of Michael Lecour, who penned the below description:

> During the 1960s, students at St. Michael's College School in Toronto had an opportunity

> to come in contact with a very special man named Stuart Lawson. Once exposed to this man, you could sense a special quality about him. Given time to reflect, you realized that what made him special was his attitude towards life. Mr. Lawson was an energetic, intelligent and multi-talented person. When asked "How are you today?" he would pause, look you straight in the eye, and confidently say "Never better!"

Mr. Lawson believed that each day of his life was better than the one before. Each day was an opportunity to meet and conquer new challenges. The statement echoed his happiness to be alive, active, caring, and thinking. He took nothing for granted. He was never too busy to help others, or to show interest in their projects, or to let you know that he loved his wife and family. The "Never Better" philosophy and way of life allowed him to enjoy all 85 active years of his life. His attitude allowed him to confidently work alongside labourers, exceptional athletes, and powerful businessmen and businesswomen, yet treat all with equal respect and dignity.

By expressing this "Never Better" philosophy, people exhibit an unqualified joy for living, a special ability to meet daily challenges and a love for family, friends, and co-workers.

This approach means that they are eager, caring, motivated, and determined to make each day "Never Better."

LESSON NOTES

Never Better

LESSON 11

Choose to Live Your Life – *Always*

This last point need not be deliberated on. It's the ultimate point.

Choose to live your life:

- By your attitude in the face of real personal challenges … which are often not of your making.
- By your perspective … to view it as you wish to see it – not as it is prescribed to you.
- By dreaming and creating possibilities in your mind that seem unachievable and unattainable.
- By writing … writing down and sharing with the world the dreams inside your head. This is your ability to take charge of your life and write your own final chapters.
- By your decisions to think and to execute. As Yoda said: "Do or do not; there is no try."

- By your decision to smile and laugh and share your light and joy with the world, and with those who you cross on your unique path.
- To never give up (when one clear option is that you do).
- To get up … when it is so easy not to, and ...
- To dress up when it seems silly and you're not going anywhere.
- To show up … even if it's across the street to an empty coffee shop to buy a coffee for yourself and donuts for the staff.

"If you really want to escape the things that harass you, what you're needing is not to be in a different place but to be a different person."
SENECA

LESSON NOTES

Choose to Live Your Life – *Always*

ABOUT CHRIS MACLEOD

Chris was born in Montreal and raised in Saskatchewan. He obtained a BA in religious studies and political science from the University of Regina. He then attended McGill University to study at the Institute of Islamic Studies for two years, prior to pursuing his law degree at the University of Saskatchewan.

He articled and practiced law in Hamilton, Ontario, from 2000 to 2010. From there he founded the law firm Cambridge LLP with two of his dearest friends, now his law partners Jon Giacomelli and Adam Cappelli.

He has been a fierce advocate for patients who need access to life-sustaining medications or treatments, founding the not-for-profit organization Canadian Cystic Fibrosis Treatment Society to assist in carrying out this work.

He has spent years working collaboratively with others on the protection of Canadians abroad, including pressing the Canadian and foreign governments when a Canadian citizen is detained overseas and their fundamental human rights are being violated. Chris and the team at Ofelas Group rise to the challenge and seek the release and return of these individuals back to Canada.

ACKNOWLEDGEMENTS

This book would not have been possible without the support of my family and friends, and the inspiration of the hundreds of individuals that I have met and known over the years who fought courageous battles to keep the breath of life. Some are still with us. Sadly, too many amazing souls didn't make it to the finish line.

The medical teams at Royal University Hospital in Saskatoon, McMaster University Medical Centre in Hamilton, Montreal Children's Hospital, and St. Michael's Hospital in Toronto have provided exceptional care over the years. I wouldn't be here if it weren't for their care. The doctors, nurses, physiotherapists, and every other professional on the medical teams at these hospitals made sure I walked out the front door and wasn't carried out the back.

Thanks to my friends from every walk of life that I have met and that have stayed with me and ultimately worked with me to secure access to a life-saving medical treatment. They were always there to talk about the dreams and plans for the future we had for ourselves and our country.

Thanks to Adam Cappelli and Jon Giacomelli with whom I founded Cambridge LLP. I couldn't ask for two better friends and amazing partners in law and business. They didn't flinch when I was on the brink.

To Dennis Mills, Scott Fairley, Dea Cappelli, Peter O'Brien, Patti Tweed, Bill Christiansen, Ashley Olah, Troy Davies, and my mom and dad, who all reviewed and assisted with editing this book. Doug Anweiler has been an incredible friend from the dark days at St. Mike's up to and including making this book happen. Wade Gilpin, Brianna Petz, and David Schurer at Sherpa Creative who did an amazing job on the book design, and thanks to Siobhan O'Connell for fact-checking and assistance with sourcing quotes. And thank you to everyone who reviewed the book and provided words of encouragement to others, that they take the time to read this book. Your praise for this undertaking means a lot to me.

During this time of a global pandemic, when everyone is concerned about their health and the health of their family and friends, I hope that this manual and these lessons learned in the trenches of a healthcare crisis provide a measure of comfort.

PAYING IT FORWARD

As is evident from the stories told in the book, literally dozens upon dozens of individuals took time out of their lives to help me get back on my feet so I could live mine. I am forever grateful.

Individuals with a health condition are required to place their effort and energy to focus and cultivate resiliency. But what they also need is a treatment or a cure for the condition they have.

In my case, a treatment came along just in the nick of time. But that treatment was discovered through expensive scientific research and development. Much of the funding for that research comes from charities and not-for-profits who are desperate for a cure or treatment for their loved one who has a life-threatening condition.

CF Canada has for decades worked with post-secondary institutions across Canada in a campaign called "Shinerama." Students from universities and colleges across the country shine shoes on a given day during their orientation week and raise money for CF research. Millions of dollars have been raised by students offering to shine the shoes of strangers for any donation of change they may have in their pocket. It started in 1964 and to date has brought in approximately 29 million dollars that can be put toward research and development for a treatment or a cure.

It doesn't stop at shining shoes. Families and individuals that have faced health challenges must first ensure their mindset is such that they can cultivate resiliency to beat the odds that have been stacked against them. Individuals also want to work on the big picture of eliminating suffering from the life of their loved one or from their own life. That can only be done with a treatment plan. It requires R&D, innovation and medication. That requires money to fund and years of trial and error to determine what might work and what won't.

Bake sales, swim-a-thons, bike-a-thons, marathons, the Man In Motion World Tour: the list of what has been undertaken is as powerful as it long. They raised across charities immense amounts of resources.

It's nickels and cents that compounded together that make a difference.

Every purchase from the website **www.beatingtheodds.ca** will allocate 10% of the sale to a charity or not-for-profit organization that advocates for patients or funds research and innovation. We will start with a list of charities we know but if you would like us to add one so we can donate to that, please advise. We can be reached at **chris@beatingtheodds.ca**

I have no idea how much we might generate to help, but I do know that change compounds whether you're cultivating resiliency or building a war chest to innovate a life-saving medicine like the one I am on.

We have set up on the **www.beatingtheodds.ca** website a link that lets you purchase a book and advise us which of our listed organizations you would like us to allocate 10% of the sale proceeds to. If you don't see the health charity that you would like to give to, please give us a call. We will consider adding more if there are requests to do so.

RECOMMENDED BOOKS AND MEDIA

Books:

50 Cent and Robert Greene. 2009. *The 50th Law.* New York: HarperCollins.

Aurelius, Marcus. 2006. *Meditations.* Translated and edited by Martin Hammond. London: Penguin Books.

Burchard, Brendon. 2017. *High Performance Habits: How Extraordinary People Became That Way.* United States: Hay House, Inc.

Cardone, Grant. 2011. *The 10X Rule: The Only Difference Between Success and Failure.* Hoboken, NY: John Wiley & Sons, Inc.

Clear, James. 2018. *Atomic Habits: An Easy & Proven Way to Build Good Habits & Break Bad Ones.* New York: Avery, an imprint of Penguin Random House.

Collier, Robert. 2013. *The Secret of the Ages.* New York: Start Publishing LLC. (Original work published in 1926).

Ferriss, Tim. 2016. *Tools of Titans: The Tactics, Routines, and Habits of Billionaires, Icons, and World-Class Performers.* Boston: Houghton Mifflin Harcourt.

Frankl, Viktor. 2006. *Man's Search for Meaning*. Boston, MA: Beacon Press. (Original work published in German, 1947).

Godin, Seth. 2010. *Linchpin: Are You Indispensable?* New York: Portfolio, an imprint of Penguin Books.

Goggins, David. 2018. *Can't Hurt Me: Master Your Mind and Defy the Odds*. United States: Lioncrest Publishing.

Grover, Tim S., and Shari Lesser Wenk. 2014. *Relentless: From Good to Great to Unstoppable*. New York: Scribner.

Hardy, Darren. 2010. *The Compound Effect: Jumpstart Your Income, Your Life, Your Success*. New York: Hachette Go, an imprint of Hachette Books.

Hill, Napoleon. 1937. *Think and Grow Rich*. United States: The Ralston Society.

Holiday, Ryan. 2014. *The Obstacle Is the Way: The Timeless Art of Turning Trials into Triumph*. New York: Portfolio, an imprint of Penguin Books.

Kushner, Harold S. 1981. *When Bad Things Happen to Good People*. New York: Schocken Books.

Lang, Amanda. 2017. *The Beauty of Discomfort: How What We Avoid is What We Need*. Harper Collins

Maxwell, John C. 2008. *Make Today Count: The Secret of Your Success is Determined by Your Daily Agenda.* Nashville, TN: Center Street.

Peters, Tom. 2012. *The Little Big Things: 163 Ways to Pursue Excellence.* New York: Harper Business.

Robbins, Tony, and Peter Mallouk. 2018. *Unshakeable: Your Financial Freedom Playbook.* New York: Simon & Schuster.

Rohn, Jim. 2012. *My Philosophy for Successful Living.* Melrose, FL: No Dream Too Big Publishing.

Rohr, Richard. 2016. *The Divine Dance: The Trinity and Your Transformation.* New Kensington, PA: Whitaker House.

Rohr, Richard. 2019. *The Universal Christ: How a Forgotten Reality Can Change Everything We See, Hope For, and Believe.* New York: Convergent Books.

Seneca, Lucio Anneo. 1997. *Dialogues and Letters.* Translated and edited by C. D. N. Costa. London: Penguin Books.

Sharma, Robin, 2018. *The 5AM Club: Own Your Morning. Elevate Your Life.* Harper Collins

Willink, Jocko, and Leif Babin. 2015. *Extreme Ownership: How U.S. Navy Seals Lead and Win.* New York: St. Martin's Press.

Media:

Clear, James. "Great Talks Most People Have Never Heard." Accessed April 18, 2021. **https://jamesclear.com/great-speeches**

MotivationalGrid. 2016. "When You Are About To Give Up – Motivational Video Speeches Compilation 1 HOUR." November 1, 2016. YouTube video, 57:40. **https://www.youtube.com/watch?v=7fSLbC-1b0Q**

Motiversity. 2016. "Best Motivational Speech Compilation Ever #3 - WAKE UP – 30-Minute Motivation Video #3". October 10, 2016. YouTube video, 30:17. **https://www.youtube.com/watch?v=FRk4PE5G-hoU**

Steindl-Rast, David. 2013. "Want to be happy? Be grateful." Filmed June 2013. TED video, 14:17. **https://www.ted.com/talks/david_steindl_rast_want_to_be_happy_be_grateful**

www.jamesclear.com is a well-organized and terrific resource for articles on habit formation. He has an ongoing project where he is listing and providing a link to "Great Talks Most People Have Never Heard of." It is a terrific resource. He also has a weekly Thursday bulletin called 3:2:1. 3 ideas from James Clear. 2 quotes from others and 1 question for you. It's free to subscribe and worth the short interruption.

Tom Bilyeu is the founder of **www.impacttheory.com**. He does an amazing job interviewing some of the brightest minds and most energetic people out there. He draws out life lessons from each person he interviews.

www.motiversity.com I would frequently go to YouTube and watch videos from this site. I love many of the speakers. People like Walter Bond former NBA player, William Hollis and Billy Alsbrooks and many others. Sometimes when you're too sick to read, or to move, it's time to let your ears and eyes do the work. Find motivation, inspiration from others who have faced challenges and overcome incredible obstacles when the odds were clearly against them.

NOTES